Dao

Cultivation

I

Vitaly Filbert

Daoist Cultivation
道家修炼

Fundamental Theory
And
Basic Philosophy

Book 1

Second Edition

2025

Daoist Cultivation Press

Los Angeles, CA, USA

Copyright © 2021, 2025 Vitaly Filbert

This book is not intended to replace a Teacher and provides general information on the topics discussed. The author and publisher disclaim any liability or loss, personal or other, as a result of the information or content in this book. The information in this book is for educational purposes only.

Contents

Foreword to the Second Edition

Since the publication of the first edition of *Daoist Cultivation, Book 1: Fundamental Theory and Basic Philosophy*, readers and students from various backgrounds have found within its pages a practical and deeply meaningful guide to Daoist thought and the path of self-cultivation.

This **Second Edition** builds upon that foundation — expanding and refining the original content to offer a more complete expression of the tradition. New chapters delve into the nature of **Ling Qi (靈氣)**, **Hunran Yi Qi (渾然一氣)**, and the **Levels of External Qi**, while key areas such as **Xing and Ming cultivation**, the **Three Treasures**, and **Daoist Cosmological Unfolding** have been significantly deepened.

Throughout the revision process, great care has been taken to integrate wisdom from classical texts such as the *Dao De Jing*, the *Xiuzhen Tu* (修真圖), and Wang Chongyang's *Fifteen Discourses Establishing the Teaching*. Original Chinese terminology has been preserved and explained where necessary, ensuring both linguistic and philosophical accuracy.

At the heart of this edition remains the intention that inspired the first: to provide a clear, grounded, and authentic entryway into the world of Daoist cultivation — a way of living and transforming that is as relevant today as it was for the sages of old.

This book is intended not as a theoretical presentation, but as a **guide to practice**, inviting you to enter the Gate of all Marvelous-Mysterious and begin walking the Way.

May your study be fruitful, and your journey harmonious.

Editor's Note on the Second Edition

This **Second Edition** of *Daoist Cultivation, Book 1* represents a substantial evolution from the first. It is not simply revised — it is restructured, clarified, and expanded in nearly every chapter.

What's New and Improved:

- **Expanded Depth**: Concepts like **Three Treasures (Jing, Qi, Shen)**, the **Three Dantian**, and the **Central Channel (Zhong Mai)** are explored with new depth and structure.

- **Classical Sources**: Original teachings from key Daoist scriptures and diagrams — including *Xiuzhen Tu*, *Taijitu Shuo*, and the *Fifteen Discourses* — are integrated directly into the theoretical framework.

- **New Content**: Entire chapters have been added, such as **Levels of External Qi**, **Ling Qi**, **Hunran Yi Qi**, and an updated look at **Daoist Cosmology** that bridges inner alchemy with the structure of the universe.

- **Terminological Clarity**: The edition consistently distinguishes between Pre-Heaven and Post-Heaven energies, clarifies key terms in Chinese, and unifies the language used throughout.

- **Visual and Conceptual Refinement**: Diagrams, tables, and flowcharts are used to make complex concepts intuitive, especially for readers new to the tradition.

This edition marks the natural maturing of the work. It follows the same principle that underlies all Daoist cultivation: **what begins must be nourished, refined, and brought to completion.**

May this revised volume serve as a more luminous lamp for those walking the Way.

Foreword

Daoism is one of the oldest living traditions in the world, its roots extending back more than five thousand years. That it continues to thrive today — in temples, in quiet mountain hermitages, in modern cities, and within the hearts of countless practitioners — is a powerful testament to its depth, clarity, and timeless relevance. Daoism has endured not because it clings to the past, but because it reveals something essential and unchanging about the nature of life itself.

In modern China, there are a wide variety of self-cultivation systems, each emphasizing different goals and methods. These systems can generally be grouped into several broad paths: Therapeutic or Medical Qigong; Wushu Qigong and the internal training methods associated with martial arts; and the more spiritually oriented traditions of Daoism, Buddhism, and Confucianism. While distinct in their approaches, all of these traditions draw on deep reservoirs of Chinese cosmology, philosophy, and energetic practice.

The influence of Daoism — along with Buddhism and Confucianism — has permeated nearly every domain of Chinese culture. Its presence can be felt not only in religion and philosophy, but also in medicine, psychology, governance, science, painting, music, poetry, martial arts, feng shui, architecture, and even garden design. The worldview it offers is not confined to temples or scriptures; it flows through the very fabric of everyday life.

Yet despite this profound impact, reliable and comprehensive resources on Daoist cultivation in English remain relatively rare. Most available texts focus either on historical overviews or simplified exercises, often lacking the subtle philosophical depth and technical precision that define the authentic tradition.

One of the main challenges in translating Daoist knowledge is the nature of the classical texts themselves. Much of Daoism's core philosophy is recorded in *Wenyan* (文言), an ancient literary style that is terse, poetic, and often deliberately ambiguous. Even among native Chinese speakers, *Wenyan* is difficult to master — and for non-native readers, its layered meanings can remain entirely out of reach. Moreover, Daoism makes frequent use of esoteric terminology, symbolic imagery, and metaphors drawn from nature, alchemy, and inner experience. These are not easily understood through intellectual study alone; they require lived experience and often the guidance of an accomplished teacher or lineage holder.

Traditionally, Daoism is attributed to the sage Lao Zi (老子), who is believed to have lived sometime between the 5th and 3rd centuries BCE. He is most well-known for composing the *Dao De Jing* (道德经), a concise yet profoundly mysterious text that continues to inspire and challenge seekers around the world. With over a thousand translations and interpretations, the *Dao De Jing* is widely regarded as the foundational scripture of Daoist philosophy.

However, many modern renditions of this classic tend to interpret it through a philosophical, poetic, or even political lens — often omitting the rich depth of its alchemical meaning. In this context, the companion volume *Dao De Jing: The Dao of Inner Alchemy* (Book 15 in this series) was written to restore the original Neidan (Internal Alchemy) perspective of the text. That book provides a practical and symbolic commentary for cultivators seeking to understand the *Dao De Jing* not merely as abstract wisdom, but as a guide to personal transformation through Daoist internal practice.

Another pivotal figure in Daoist lore is the Yellow Emperor, Huang Di (黄帝), a legendary sovereign said to have lived in the 26th century BCE. Although modern historians classify him as a mythological figure, Daoist tradition credits him with transmitting many early teachings on medicine, cosmology, alchemy, and self-cultivation. His legacy is not defined by historical accuracy but by the symbolic role he plays — as a primordial sage-king who harmonized Heaven and Earth and laid the foundations for the Way of cultivation.

The earliest Chinese writing, known as *Jiaguwen* (甲骨文) — the oracle bone script — only appeared around the 14th to 11th centuries BCE. From this, we can see that much of what is attributed to Huang Di belongs to the realm of sacred mythology rather than verifiable history. Yet for the Daoist practitioner, this is of little concern. The myths of Daoism are not intended to serve as literal records; they are vessels for truth. Their purpose is to point beyond surface understanding and evoke something deeper — something that stirs the intuition and leads the sincere seeker inward.

It is in this spirit that Daoism is sometimes referred to as *Huang-Lao Xue* (黃老学) — "The Teaching of Huang [Di] and Lao [Zi]." This name captures the dual nature of the tradition: a blend of mythic wisdom and philosophical clarity, of cosmic vision and practical insight. To walk the Daoist path is not simply to study an old philosophy, but to enter into a living current — one that flows quietly through the center of all things.

Introduction

The Daoist School *Zhen Dao Pai* (真道派), or "School of the True Way," is a living tradition of spiritual and physical cultivation, rooted in the ancient teachings of Daoist Masters and Immortals. What we preserve and pass on today is not a reconstructed theory, but a direct and experiential lineage that has withstood time because it works — not only for health and clarity of mind, but also for deep spiritual realization.

From the very beginning, all methods in our School are based on the principle of *Xing Ming Shuang Xiu* (性命双修) — the simultaneous cultivation of original nature, body and life-force. This approach reflects the heart of the Daoist Way: not escaping the world, but refining ourselves within it. Students may begin with simple goals — improving their health, calming the mind, gaining balance — but for those who wish to go further, the path naturally deepens into inner alchemy, consciousness refinement, and ultimately, the return to one's Original Nature.

The training program includes essential Daoist practices: *Qigong* (energy cultivation), *Dao Yin, Taiji Quan,* and *Xing Yi Quan* (body-mind integration), *Tuna* (breath refinement), and most importantly, *Neidan* (內丹), the core alchemical art of Daoist transformation. These practices are not random collections of techniques — they are part of a coherent system that, when followed with sincerity and perseverance, can carry the practitioner to the highest peaks of inner development.

The origins of *Zhen Dao Pai* are attributed to some of the most legendary figures in Daoist history: the Immortal Lü Dongbin, and his disciples Wang Chongyang and Liu Haichan. Their teachings became the foundation for a complete system that we continue to practice today.

By the time I met my teacher, Grandmaster Lü Shiyang (吕實陽), in 1998, I already had a strong foundation in Daoist philosophy and had been practicing several related methods on my own. I knew what I was looking for — not vague inspiration or general spiritual guidance, but a living transmission of the authentic Daoist path. When I encountered his teaching, I recognized it immediately. It was exactly what I had been searching for.

I went on to spend extensive time in China, participating in retreats and engaging in the traditional, disciplined study of *Neidan* under his close guidance. This was not casual or conceptual learning — it was hands-on, embodied cultivation that required commitment and inner transformation. Later, I also lived and practiced in a Buddhist mountain monastery in Nepal, experiences that broadened my understanding of spiritual life and helped me appreciate the similarities and distinctions between Daoist and Buddhist teachings.

Over time, and with Master Lü Shiyang's encouragement and support, I undertook the work of organizing the knowledge I received into a clear and usable system. Traditional Daoist instruction, while deep and powerful, often relies on rigid cultural forms, coded language, and oral transmission. Much of it is not easily accessible to modern practitioners, especially those living outside of China. I wanted to make these teachings available without diluting their essence — to translate not just the words, but the spirit of the path.

The result is the current form of *Zhen Dao Pai*. It remains true to its classical roots, but is structured in a way that can meet the needs of sincere students today. Whether your focus is on restoring vitality, calming the mind, or exploring the full depths of Daoist internal alchemy, this system provides a way forward. Each student can walk their own path, at their own pace — from the foundations of health and harmony to the highest levels of inner awakening.

But one thing remains constant: the Dao responds to sincerity. The Way does not depend on belief or theory. It reveals itself through direct experience. And for those who are ready, the door is open.

The Structure of the Zhen Dao Pai System

The system of *Zhen Dao Pai* is built upon three essential components of cultivation. Together, they form a complete method of self-transformation that addresses the practitioner's body, energy, and spirit. These three units are:

真
道
派

1. **The Art of Inner Quietness and Calmness (静坐功)** — Inner Alchemy (*Neidan*)

2. **The Art of External Movement (外动功)** — Methods of working with the body

3. **The Art of Sleeping (睡功)** — Lying-down practices and dream techniques

While each of these aspects has its own purpose and unique power, the Art of Inner Quietness and Calmness is regarded as the heart of the entire system.

The Art of Inner Quietness and Calmness (静坐功)

The Art of Inner Quietness and Calmness is one of the most refined and extraordinary achievements of the Daoist tradition. It represents the culmination of countless generations of inner exploration, aimed not only at health or balance but at complete spiritual transformation.

All methods within this unit are performed in a state of stillness, most often in a seated posture with crossed legs. At the center of this system lies the practice of Daoist meditation (*Da Zuo* 打坐), also known as Sitting in Quietness and Calmness (*Jing Zuo* 静坐). These practices are often referred to collectively as Inner Alchemy (*Neidan* 內丹), and it is through them that profound internal changes can occur — in the body, the energy system, and the spirit of the practitioner.

It is important to note that Inner Alchemy is fundamentally different from ordinary Qigong. Qigong methods typically work with ordinary *Qi*, focusing on strengthening physical health, emotional stability, and general vitality. These are valuable and effective in their own right. But *Neidan* goes much deeper. It works not with ordinary *Qi*, but with Original Qi — the prenatal, undifferentiated energy that lies at the root of existence. This is the energy of creation itself, and it is through the refinement of this subtle essence that one's True Nature can be realized.

This is why Inner Alchemy is considered the core and foundation of Practical Daoism. It is not simply a set of seated exercises or energy techniques. It is a complete spiritual path — one that leads, step by step, from the ordinary human condition toward the realization of the True Original Nature. The ancient teachings of *Neidan* are preserved and taught within the *Zhen Dao Pai* lineage, making it a full system of Daoist cultivation — not merely a school of Qigong, but a transmission of the living Dao.

The Three Vehicles of Inner Alchemy

The mastery of Inner Quietness and Calmness unfolds through three Vehicles — stages of realization, each representing a different level of attainment along the path of internal alchemy:

1. **The Lesser Vehicle** – The Mastery of **Human Immortals**

2. **The Middle Vehicle** – The Mastery of **Earth Immortals**

3. **The Great Vehicle** – The Mastery of **Celestial Immortals**

Each Vehicle contains a structured progression of levels and corresponding methods. This level-based system was established by Grandmaster Lü Dongbin around a thousand years ago and has been transmitted through generations to the present day.

These three stages do not merely represent symbolic ideals. They are concrete phases of development, marked by real energetic, psychological, and spiritual transformations. Each Vehicle refines a deeper layer of the self, gradually dissolving the separation between the practitioner and the Dao.

The Art of External Moving (外动功)

The Art of External Moving is both a foundation and a preparation for the Art of Inner Quietness and Calmness. These two aspects of training are not in opposition — rather, they illuminate and support one another. External movement prepares the body, energy, and consciousness for stillness. Stillness, in turn, reveals the full depth and subtlety of movement.

Although this unit includes work with Life Force (*Qi*) and consciousness, the methods it contains are not classified as *Inner Alchemy* (*Neidan*). For this reason, it is referred to as "external." But this does not mean the work is superficial — only that it belongs to the earlier, more accessible stages of cultivation. When practiced with attention and precision, it leads to a harmonious circulation of Yin and Yang, the refinement of *Jing*, *Qi*, and *Shen*, and the development of a strong, stable body and energy system.

This unit encompasses a wide range of dynamic and static practices, including:

- **Dao Yin** — methods of guiding energy and stretching the body

- **Health Preservation and Healing Techniques** — systems for restoring internal balance

- **Wushu (Taiji Quan and Xing Yi Quan)** — traditional martial arts for body, energy, and spirit

- **The Art of Exchanging Qi with Natural Sources** — absorbing and harmonizing with the Qi of Heaven, Earth, Sun, Moon, stars, trees, mountains, rivers, and other natural phenomena

Wushu Mastery, for example, is a powerful tool not only for strengthening the physical body but also for awakening and refining the energy system and consciousness. The specific Wushu styles studied may vary depending on the Master, but their function remains the same: to prepare the vessel of the human being for deeper alchemical transformation.

Especially in the early stages of training, it is essential for students to engage in active, embodied practice. The regulation of *Jing*, *Qi*, and *Shen* must begin with a solid foundation in movement. Neglecting this foundational unit — or skipping it entirely — often leads to stagnation and imbalance later on. A weak or undeveloped physical body, an unrefined energy system, and scattered consciousness will ultimately obstruct the deeper progress of Inner Alchemy.

The path must be built upon both dynamic and static practice. This is the most harmonious and complete Way.

The Dao does not favor lopsided development. One cannot cultivate only the mind or only the body and expect wholeness. The Art of External Moving ensures that the physical, energetic, and spiritual aspects of the practitioner develop in tandem, allowing for genuine transformation to unfold from the ground up.

The Art of Sleeping (睡功)

The **Art of Sleeping** (*Shui Gong* 睡功), also known as the "Mastership of Sleeping," was developed to allow the process of cultivation to continue during the night, even while the body is at rest. It is a method that bridges the visible and invisible, extending the work begun during the day into the realm of sleep and deep stillness. Within the Daoist tradition, this is not merely a poetic idea — it is a refined and potent practice that brings the alchemical process into a more subtle and transformative dimension.

Many of the methods in this unit are attributed to the legendary Daoist Immortal **Chen Tuan** (陳摶), also known as **Chen Xi Yi** (陳希夷), whose profound teachings laid the foundation for sleep-based cultivation. For this reason, the **Art of Inner Quietness and Calmness** is regarded as essential preparation. Without first cultivating inner stillness, presence, and the refinement of *Qi*, one cannot properly enter or stabilize the deeper stages of sleeping practice.

In the *Zhen Dao Pai* tradition, this unit draws from several ancient Daoist texts, including:

- *Chen Tuan,* **General Instructions for the Twelve Sleep Practices of the Hua Mountains** (華山十二睡功總訣)

- *Chen Tuan,* **The Method of the Sleeping Dragon** (蟄龍法)

- *Zhang Sanfeng,* **Song of the Sleeping Dragon** (蟄龍吟)

- *Lu Dongbin,* **Verses on the Method of the Sleeping Dragon** (詠蟄龍法)

- *Wang Daoyuan,* **Discourse on Dreams** (夢說)

These foundational works are explored and translated in greater depth in *Book 13: The Daoist Art of Sleeping and Dream Cultivation,* which also offers commentary and practice guidance for modern students.

One important focus of *Shui Gong* is a particular type of alchemical work performed in the supine position — that is, lying down — in a state that appears externally as ordinary sleep, yet within which the practitioner maintains subtle awareness. This state is different from dreaming. It is characterized by deep stillness and absence of mental projection, allowing energetic transformation to occur without the interference of conscious thought. These methods are transmitted directly through dedicated retreats and seminars, where they can be taught with the necessary detail and care.

Another essential aspect of this art is the practice of spiritual dreaming. This is not merely about controlling or navigating dreams, but about working directly with the *Hun* (魂), the ethereal soul, and the *Shen* (神), the spirit. Through these practices, the practitioner gradually becomes aware of the subtle mechanics of dream and consciousness. The ultimate goal of spiritual dreaming is to comprehend the true nature of the dream itself — to awaken within illusion, and recognize that what we perceive, both in dreams and in waking life, arises from the same inner source. In this way, spiritual dreaming becomes a gateway to direct insight into the illusory nature of appearances and the deeper truth that lies behind them.

One of the remarkable features of *Shui Gong* is the possibility of learning from one's Master during sleep. In certain cases, the practitioner may receive teachings in dreams, either from their current embodied teacher or from a Master they have never met in waking life but are spiritually connected to. These dream-transmissions may include subtle energetic methods, symbolic instructions, or clear experiential guidance. When the practitioner

13

has sufficient inner stillness and Qi reserve, this knowledge can be consciously integrated upon waking.

With this unit, *Zhen Dao Pai* preserves a complete cycle of practice: waking, meditating, moving, and sleeping — all transformed into fields of cultivation. The practitioner does not train only while seated or only while moving, but also while resting and dreaming. In this way, the Art of Sleeping completes the sacred rhythm of the Daoist path — allowing the spirit to grow in silence, in stillness, and in the subtle places where the mind cannot follow.

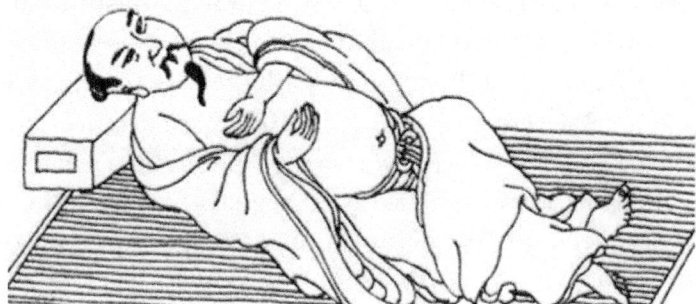

Summary of the Three Arts of Zhen Dao Pai

Art	Chinese Term	Primary Focus	Practice Forms	Key Outcomes
Art of Inner Quietness and Calmness	静坐功 (*Jing Zuo Gong*)	Inner Alchemy (*Neidan*) — cultivation in stillness and seated meditation	Sitting meditation, Qi cultivation, work with Original *Jing*, *Qi*, and *Shen*	Awakening of Original Nature, transformation of body–Qi–Spirit, Unity with Dao
Art of External Moving	外动功 (*Wai Dong Gong*)	Manifestation of the Source through movement; dynamic and static training for body, energy, and consciousness	Dao Yin, Taiji, Xing Yi, health preservation, Qi exchange with nature	Foundation building, Yin–Yang harmonization, strengthening of the body, energy refinement, preparation for Neidan
Art of Sleeping	睡功 (*Shui Gong*)	Continuation of cultivation during rest; dream-based spiritual work	Supine alchemical practice, spiritual dreaming, dream awareness, learning from Master through dreams	Spirit (*Shen*) development, comprehension of the dream's true nature, deepened access to inner realms

Basic
Terminology

Qigong (氣功)

"Qigong" is probably the most well-known word associated with Chinese systems of self-development. It's widely used in discussions about health, energy, and meditation — but like many popular terms, its meaning is often misunderstood or oversimplified. Let's take a closer look and clarify what it truly represents.

The term **Qigong** (氣功) is made up of two Chinese characters:

- **Qi** (氣): usually translated as *Life Force* or *Vital Energy*

- **Gong** (功): meaning *effort, achievement, mastery,* or *the skill developed through diligent work*

Put together, **Qigong** can be translated as *"the skillful cultivation of Life Force"* or *"the art of working with Qi."*

More specifically, Qigong refers to a wide array of exercises aimed at restoring the natural circulation of Qi within the body, accumulating additional energy, and enhancing overall balance across all layers of the human being — physical (body), emotional (feelings), and mental (thoughts). It includes breathing techniques, body movements, mental focus, and sometimes visualization.

Although the term "Qigong" became widespread only in the 1960s, many Qigong practices are rooted in ancient Daoist cultivation methods that have existed for thousands of years. In earlier times, these methods were often called **Yang Sheng Fa** (养生法), meaning *"Methods of Nourishing Life."* These were frequently associated with the Daoist tradition, though they were also practiced in other cultural and medical contexts.

Qigong is now practiced throughout China and around the world, largely due to its excellent therapeutic results. Many sequences

17

can be learned by people of all ages and physical conditions, making it a valuable and accessible entry point into the world of energetic cultivation.

However, the growing popularity of Qigong has also brought confusion and misinformation. Because of a lack of historical knowledge or proper guidance, many people approach Qigong as a spiritual path, hoping to realize their highest potential through exercises that were primarily created for physical health and energetic balance. This is a fundamental misunderstanding. While Qigong is powerful and beneficial, it is not the same as **Neidan**, or Daoist Inner Alchemy.

To use an analogy: if you want to go to Mars, you need a spacecraft — not a car. A car is useful, but not for interplanetary travel. In the same way, Qigong is a reliable and effective vehicle for improving health and calming the mind, but it was not designed for the higher work of spiritual transmutation. Expecting the results of Daoist alchemy from ordinary Qigong methods is not only unrealistic — it can also lead to self-deception and stagnation.

That said, I have great respect for Qigong, and many forms of it are included in the **Building the Foundation** stage of the Zhen Dao Pai system. There are countless Qigong practices that appear simple on the outside, yet contain deep layers of refinement for those who know how to work internally. The key lies in the inner work. Without it, even the most graceful movements become little more than soft gymnastics.

But when practiced correctly and consistently, Qigong allows you to:

- Learn to deeply relax both body and mind — especially important in the overstimulated modern world

- Enter a state of inner harmony and mental clarity

- Cultivate a peaceful mood through calm breathing and fluid movement

- Develop "collected relaxation" — a state of awareness combined with softness and internal strength

- Improve work efficiency, focus, and endurance

- Gain better control over emotions and internal states

In addition, most Qigong practices require no special equipment, environment, or athletic ability. They are open to anyone, regardless of age or physical condition. The keys to success are simple: sincerity, consistency, and determination. With regular practice, you will begin to feel the Qi, understand it, interact with it, and eventually guide its flow. You'll learn to clear blockages, absorb energy from the environment, and store it in the body's internal reservoirs — especially the Dantians.

Over time, your body will become more resilient, your mind more stable, and many imbalances may simply fade away. Qigong is not a shortcut to spiritual enlightenment — but it is a precious method for establishing the health, sensitivity, and inner awareness necessary for those who wish to go deeper.

The Main Types of Qigong

While all Qigong works with *Qi* (Life Force), there are different branches based on their purpose and method. Understanding these distinctions helps prevent confusion — especially when Qigong is mistaken for advanced spiritual practice.

Type of Qigong	Focus	Purpose	Common Examples
Medical Qigong	Restoring balance and healing illness	Clearing energetic blockages, supporting organ health, treating physical or emotional issues	Hospital-based Qigong therapy, healing sequences
Martial Qigong	Enhancing strength, endurance, and internal power	Supporting martial arts training and developing explosive force (Fa Jin 發勁)	Iron Shirt, Iron Palm, special martial arts training
Spiritual Qigong	Cultivating awareness, calming the mind, and elevating consciousness	Preparing the body and mind for meditation and deeper internal work	Basic meditation, breathing forms, work with ordinary *Jing*, *Qi*, and *Shen*

Note: Many modern Qigong systems mix elements from all three types, but it's important to know what a particular method was originally designed to do.

In Daoist cultivation, Qigong belongs primarily to the preparatory phase known as Building the Foundation, which supports—but does not replace Neidan.

Tuna (吐纳): Daoist Breathing Techniques

Tuna (吐纳) is the Daoist art of breathing — a core technique that has been practiced and refined for thousands of years. The term Tuna literally means *"to expel and to receive"* — referring to the process of releasing the impure (*turbid Qi*) and drawing in the pure (*clear Qi*). This reflects the foundational Daoist principle of purification and renewal through natural cycles.

No one doubts the importance of breathing. It is central not only to life but to the health and functioning of the entire body. In Daoist thought, however, breathing is not merely a biological necessity — it is a bridge between the visible and invisible aspects of the self. The way we breathe directly affects our physical body, our emotions, and our mental state. This is why Tuna holds a distinct and honored place in the Daoist tradition.

We can easily observe how breath reflects emotional states. When someone is angry, frightened, or agitated, their breathing becomes shallow, fast, and erratic. When calm and peaceful, the breath deepens and slows. In Daoism, this interrelationship is often summarized through the triad: Breath — Heart — Mind. If breathing is disturbed, the heart becomes unstable, and the mind restless. But if the breath is calm and harmonious, it helps stabilize the emotions and quiet the mind.

Breathing is also intricately tied to the movement of **Qi** within the body. Through breath, we not only take in oxygen, but also absorb what Daoists call "external Qi" — the subtle energy of nature and the cosmos. Using correct breathing techniques, we can refine this Qi, guide its circulation through the channels, and store it in key energy centers such as the Dantians. As a result, breathing becomes both a health practice and an energetic method for building and stabilizing the internal landscape.

For these reasons, Tuna is essential in the stage of Building the Foundation. Proper breathing provides the groundwork for inner peace, energetic balance, and mental clarity. Without regulating

21

the breath, it becomes difficult — and sometimes impossible — to enter deep states of practice. That's why this phase must be taken seriously and not rushed or overlooked.

Daoist tradition contains a vast array of breathing techniques. These vary widely depending on the intended purpose — from healing illness, to calming the mind, to accumulating Qi, or preparing the body for advanced inner alchemy. The methods differ in:

- **Breathing style**: forward, reverse, abdominal, whole-body, sighing, or skin breathing

- **Rhythm**: fast, slow, patterned, or variable

- **Breath retention**: whether breath is held after inhalation, exhalation, or both — or not held at all

- **Internal focus**: whether attention is placed on Dantians, meridians, organs, or external elements

- **Dynamic elements**: some techniques include body movements, hand positions, or visualizations

- **Sound**: some forms use specific sounds or vibrations to move or purify energy

Among the most advanced is the method known as Embryonic Breathing (*Tai Xi* 胎息), in which the practitioner gradually ceases to breathe through the lungs in the ordinary way. The breath becomes so subtle it is almost imperceptible. In deep states of this practice, the heart slows down dramatically, and may even appear to stop. This level of Tuna is associated with prolonged meditative absorption — sometimes lasting for days, weeks, or even longer — and is only accessible at high stages of spiritual cultivation.

Historically, breathing techniques have been carefully recorded in Daoist texts since at least the 4th–3rd centuries BCE. Ancient manuals even describe when in the day to perform specific breathing practices and what effects they will produce. The precision of these records suggests that the methods were already mature and systematized at the time of their writing — pointing to an even older lineage of knowledge.

One of the most important classical sources is Ge Hong's *Baopu Zi* (抱朴子), *"The Master Who Embraces Simplicity"*, written in the early 4th century CE. In it, Ge Hong explains that those who master breathing and the regulation of Qi can acquire extraordinary abilities — such as healing diseases, influencing natural forces, and fearlessness in the face of wild animals. While such claims may sound mythical to the modern mind, in Daoist language they express the immense potential of harmonizing breath, spirit, and nature.

In short, Tuna is not optional. It is a vital, living art. When practiced correctly, Daoist breathing becomes more than a tool — it becomes a doorway. A subtle portal through which the ordinary breath is transformed into something luminous, spacious, and profoundly healing.

Types of Tuna (Daoist Breathing Techniques)

Daoist breathing (*Tuna*) includes a wide range of methods developed for different goals. Below are some of the main types, often used during the Building the Foundation stage — and sometimes far beyond.

Breathing Type	Description	Purpose
Forward Breathing	Inhale expands abdomen, exhale contracts it	Calms the nervous system, restores basic Qi flow
Reverse Breathing	Inhale contracts abdomen, exhale expands it	Builds inner pressure, used in martial and energetic training
Abdominal Breathing	Deep, slow breath focused in the lower Dantian	Strengthens energy center, promotes grounding and internal stillness
Embryonic Breathing	Ultra-refined breath; natural, invisible, and sometimes non-physical	Prepares for deep meditation and long internal stillness
Skin/Body Breathing	Absorbing Qi through the pores or whole body awareness	Merges self with natural energy fields; advanced energetic integration
Sighing/ Mixed Breathing	Combining natural sighs or mixed techniques with awareness	Helps release emotional stagnation and adjust internal flow

Note: Techniques may include breath retention, sound, movement, or visualization, depending on the intended function.

Reminder: The key to all breathing practices is *not the form alone, but the quality of internal awareness.* Without correct inner engagement, even refined techniques lose their depth and power.

Dao Yin (導引): Guiding the Body, Harmonizing the Spirit

Dao Yin (導引), meaning *"guiding and stretching,"* is one of the oldest physical arts within the Daoist tradition. While it appears to be a set of movements aimed at improving flexibility and health, its true purpose reaches much deeper: to free the body from deep internal suppressions, activate the energetic pathways, and cultivate a profound connection between body, energy, spirit, and the forces of nature.

Dao Yin is not simply exercise. It is a physical, energetic, and spiritual practice designed to release tension, awaken perception, and restore the natural harmony of the human being. Its movements guide the Qi, open the meridians, balance Yin and Yang, and refine the inner landscape. At the same time, it nourishes **virtue**, dissolves inner obstructions, and fosters the development of a clear and centered consciousness.

Dao Yin works on multiple levels:

- **Physically**, it strengthens and softens the body, increases mobility, and enhances blood circulation. Special focus is given to the **spine**, the structural core of the body, and to opening key joints — the hips, knees, and ankles — which are essential for preparing to sit comfortably in meditation.

- **Energetically**, it clears and opens the channels, elaborates the internal "gates" (*guan* 關), harmonizes internal and external Qi, and increases the practitioner's overall energy potential.

- **Spiritually**, it cultivates stillness within movement, dissolves emotional blockages, and encourages the rise of virtuous qualities — without which true spiritual development is impossible.

Importantly, Dao Yin should not be confused with modern forms of flexibility training. Super-flexibility or extreme mobility is not the goal. Movements are generally smooth, gentle, and circular — designed to calm the nervous system, release tension, and harmonize the breath and Qi. Relaxation and softness are often more important than visible strength or range of motion.

Dao Yin is a broad category. It includes both introductory-level exercises for basic health and flexibility, and higher-level practices focused on energetic refinement and spiritual cultivation. These exercises may be practiced in standing, sitting, or lying positions, depending on the goal. Some Dao Yin sets are primarily somatic and therapeutic, while others activate the internal Dantians, circulate energy through specific channels, and align the body with Heaven and Earth.

One of the essential features of authentic Dao Yin is the integration of internal intention (*Yi*, 意) and spiritual direction (*Shen*, 神). From the very first to the last movement, the practitioner maintains an inner awareness oriented toward the Dao — toward the Supreme Origin. This orientation transforms ordinary movement into sacred work.

In advanced Dao Yin, the practitioner learns to:

- Synchronize the **Three Dantians** (Lower, Middle, Upper)

- Connect with the energies of **Heaven, Earth, Sun, Moon,** and stars

- Harmonize **internal and external Qi**

- Refine the Spirit (*Shen*) and dissolve the ego

- Root the body, open the heart, and awaken the mind in alignment with the Dao

In this way, Dao Yin becomes more than an exercise. It becomes a gateway — a moving meditation through which the human form becomes transparent to the natural forces flowing through it. It reconnects the practitioner with the rhythm of the cosmos and lays the groundwork for higher stages of inner alchemy.

As the *Zhen Dao Pai* tradition teaches:
True Dao Yin is not about movement — it is about direction. It is about where the Spirit is going while the body moves.

Neigong (內功): The Art of Inner Work

Neigong (內功), meaning *"Inner Work"* or *"Internal Skill,"* refers to a deep and refined level of internal cultivation. Like Qigong, it involves working with the body, breath, energy, and mind — but it differs in the quality of awareness, depth of practice, and clarity of internal intention.

The boundary between Qigong and Neigong is not always fixed. The distinction often depends on the school, tradition, or teacher offering the instruction. In many modern contexts, Qigong has become a general term for any kind of health-promoting or energetically focused movement practice. As a result, some forms of Qigong may consist primarily of coordinated movements, done with limited attention to internal intention, energy flow, or deeper understanding.

By contrast, Neigong implies a more conscious and purposeful inner process. It is not just about what the body is doing — it's about what the *Yi* (intention), *Qi*, and *Shen* are doing at the same time. In Neigong, students engage with the underlying theory, understand the energetic architecture of the body, and work with specific internal mechanisms such as Dantians, meridians, and energy gates. It is a practice that requires awareness, subtlety, and internal stillness — even when the movements are external.

While Qigong may serve as an introduction or therapeutic tool, Neigong is a bridge — a transitional stage that connects outer practices with the deeper internal transformation of Neidan (Internal Alchemy). It prepares the ground for that work by refining the practitioner's energy, sharpening the mind, and stabilizing the spirit.

There are many forms of Neigong, each with its own goals:

- Some are used in martial arts to develop internal power and structure

- Others are associated with Dao Yin or Yang Sheng Fa (nourishing life) methods

- Many forms focus on energy regulation, emotional refinement, and spiritual clarity

Regardless of the form, the defining quality of Neigong is that it always turns the practitioner inward. The work is subtle. It can involve holding postures, moving slowly through precise sequences, or remaining completely still while working internally. Physical movement may be minimal, but the internal processes are rich and transformative.

A Neigong practitioner learns not just *how* to move or breathe, but *why* — and what is happening beneath the surface. They develop the ability to:

- Sense and direct Qi with precision

- Open and close energetic gates

- Link breath, intention, and energy as a unified process

- Stabilize emotional and mental fluctuations

- Cultivate presence and internal spaciousness

In this way, Neigong becomes a kind of energetic literacy — a language of awareness that prepares the practitioner for more advanced internal alchemical work. It is the place where the visible begins to dissolve into the invisible, where external effort gives way to internal transformation.

Neigong is where the work becomes real — not because it looks impressive, but because it changes what you are inside.

Neidan (內丹): The Path of Inner Alchemy

Neidan, or *Inner Alchemy*, is the crown jewel of Daoist cultivation. The term 內丹 translates literally as *"Internal Elixir,"* and refers to a profound system of inner transformation that works not only with energy and breath, but with consciousness, essence, and spirit — the deepest layers of what we are.

At its root, Neidan is based on the practice of seated meditation (*Dazuo* 打坐), specifically in a condition of motionless calm and silence (*Jingzuo* 静坐). But unlike ordinary meditation for relaxation or mindfulness, Neidan is a structured, intentional, and highly symbolic system of internal transformation whose goal is nothing less than the awakening of the Original Nature within every human being.

How Neidan Differs from Qigong

The fundamental difference between Neidan and Qigong lies in what kind of energy and consciousness they work with.

- **Qigong** generally works with Post-Heaven Qi — the energies of Heaven, Earth, and Nature. These are powerful and useful for maintaining health, emotional balance, and mental clarity.

- **Neidan**, by contrast, works with the Original Treasures — the Pre-Heaven, primordial forces that precede form:

    - **Yuan Jing** (元精) – Original Essence

    - **Yuan Qi** (元氣) – Original Energy

    - **Yuan Shen** (元神) – Original Spirit

In addition to these, Neidan also makes use of the True Qi (*Zhen Qi* 真氣) of Heaven and Earth — the undiluted forces that shape the cosmos.

These original forces are not only more subtle and powerful — they are the foundation of who we are beneath personality, memory, and ego. Working with them unlocks an entirely different dimension of cultivation. One's energy becomes stabilized, one's spirit clarified, and one's life transformed from the inside out.

The Purpose of Neidan Practice

In ordinary life, we live outwardly. Our senses and thoughts are directed toward the external world. We pursue goals, accumulate knowledge, chase comfort or success — yet this often leads to fragmentation, dissatisfaction, and confusion. We lose sight of who we are.

Neidan reverses this movement. It draws the practitioner inward — toward the essential Being at the core of one's existence. Through stillness, presence, and precise internal techniques, Neidan allows us to reconnect with our innermost nature — what Daoist texts call the Original Nature (*Xing* 性).

This return is not an escape from the world, but a reorientation. When we perceive clearly from our Original Nature, we can respond to life without distortion. The heart is clean. The mind is calm. The body is no longer in conflict with spirit. In this way, Neidan becomes the means by which we not only transform ourselves, but come to understand and live in harmony with the Dao.

The Elixir of Immortality (金丹 – Jindan)

At the center of Neidan lies the symbolic creation of the Elixir of Immortality (*Jindan* 金丹). This is not a literal substance, but a transformation that takes place within the body–mind–spirit system. By working with the Original Treasures and harmonizing them through special internal practices, the practitioner generates a unique energetic formation within the body.

This inner elixir opens not only the standard and extraordinary meridians, but also alchemical channels that exist only in deep states of cultivation. As this process unfolds, the physical body is refined, the spirit becomes luminous, and one's connection to the eternal becomes experiential — not theoretical.

This is what the Daoist tradition refers to as the process of double cultivation — the simultaneous refinement of Xing (Nature) and Ming (Life/Vitality).

Transmission and Secrecy

Because of its depth and power, the methods of Neidan were traditionally kept secret — passed orally from master to disciple in select lineages. Unlike Qigong, which is widely practiced and shared in modern times, Inner Alchemy was reserved for serious, dedicated practitioners, often requiring years of preparation before access was granted.

In the Zhen Dao Pai tradition, Inner Alchemy is the core and heart of the teaching. It is given the highest priority, and taught not merely as a set of techniques, but as a path of inner purification, spiritual clarity, and return to the Source. Special emphasis is placed on cleansing and cultivating the Heart Nature, dissolving emotional and mental obscurations, and restoring contact with the Yuan Shen — the unblemished Original Spirit.

A person who has completed this process, who has awakened their Original Nature and transcended ordinary consciousness, is traditionally called an Immortal (*Xian* 仙) — not because they escape death, but because they have realized the eternal essence that exists beyond it.

The goal of Neidan is not to become something greater — but to return to what you already are, before anything was added.

Core Structure of Neidan (Inner Alchemy)

Element	Chinese Term	Meaning / Function
Original Essence	元精 (*Yuan Jing*)	Root of physical vitality; refined into Qi
Original Energy	元氣 (*Yuan Qi*)	Source energy of life; governs transformation and circulation
Original Spirit	元神 (*Yuan Shen*)	Innate pure awareness; the spiritual light before form and identity
True Qi of Heaven & Earth	真氣 (*Zhen Qi*)	Harmonizing cosmic energy; supports higher-level integration
Elixir of Immortality	金丹 (*Jindan*)	Energetic and spiritual formation produced by refining and uniting the Original Treasures
Cultivation of Nature	性 (*Xing*)	Awakening Original Nature; comprehending the innermost essence of Being and Non-being; awakening original wisdom
Cultivation of Life/Vitality	命 (*Ming*)	Refining life force; transforming the body and energetic structure
Double Cultivation	性命雙修 (*Xing–Ming Shuang Xiu*)	Harmonizing Nature and Life; leads to realization and unity with the Dao

Comparison of Qigong, Neigong, and Neidan

Aspect	Qigong (氣功)	Neigong (內功)	Neidan (內丹)
Meaning	"Life Force Skill"	"Inner Skill / Inner Work"	"Internal Alchemy"
Focus	Health, energy flow, relaxation	Energetic refinement, internal awareness	Spiritual transformation, return to the Source
Depth of Practice	Often external with some internal aspects	Internal processes emphasized	Fully internal and symbolic-alchemical
Intention (Yi)	May or may not be consciously used	Central to guiding Qi and practice	Directs transformation of Jing → Qi → Shen → Xu (Emptiness)
Common Methods	Movement sequences, breathing, light meditation	Postural holding, breath/ Qi control, subtle intent	Stillness, meditation, work with Original Treasures
Theory Engagement	Basic or minimal	Intermediate to deep understanding of theory	Deep understanding of Daoist cosmology & self
Relationship to Alchemy	Often preparatory only	Transitional stage to deeper cultivation	Core method of Daoist spiritual alchemy
Goal	Restore health, balance emotions	Refine body-energy-mind unity	Awaken True Nature, unite with Dao

Qigong builds the base. Neigong deepens the inner structure. Neidan transforms the whole being.

Yin–Yang Theory (陰陽): The Dynamic Balance of the Universe

The Yin–Yang theory is one of the oldest and most central concepts in Daoist philosophy. While it has become a widely recognized symbol in popular culture, the true depth and subtlety of its meaning are often lost. Many have seen the Yin–Yang diagram, but few understand what it really represents — especially in the context of Daoist internal cultivation.

What Are Yin and Yang?

At its core, the Yin–Yang theory expresses the relationship between two original, complementary, and opposing forces that underlie the entire Universe. These forces are present in all things — from the cosmos to the human body, from cycles of nature to fluctuations in energy and consciousness.

- **Yin (陰)**: receptive, inward, cooling, condensing

- **Yang (陽)**: active, outward, warming, expanding

Together, these two form a cosmic polarity, not in opposition like enemies, but in creative tension. It is from their dynamic relationship that life, change, and movement arise.

To understand Dao, and to walk the path of returning to one's Original Nature, a practitioner must learn to observe and regulate the Yin and Yang forces within the body and mind — and not simply rely on abstract philosophy.

The Symbol and Its Misinterpretations

The most common image associated with Yin and Yang today is the Taiji (太極) diagram — the black-and-white "fish" in a circle, each containing a dot of the other. Taiji means *"Supreme Ultimate,"* and this symbol indeed carries profound meaning. However, this modern version of the diagram was developed only a few hundred years ago — and is not found in the most ancient Daoist texts from over 800 years ago.

This diagram is often interpreted as showing:

- Yin contains Yang, and Yang contains Yin

- There is no absolute Yin or absolute Yang

- Each force gives rise to the other in a continuous flow

This philosophical view is accurate in many respects. It encourages non-dual thinking and avoids rigid categorization. However, it becomes problematic when applied directly to Yin and Yang energies in actual Daoist cultivation.

Yin and Yang Energies Are Truly Opposite

Many people mistakenly say that Yin and Yang attract each other — but this is not accurate from the standpoint of energetic mechanics. As Daoist Master Zhang Boduan (張伯端) explained in *Wuzhen Pian*, Yin and Yang are like fire and water: they are opposite in nature, and their interactions must follow precise laws. Their mutual influence is governed not by attraction of opposites, but by resonance and rhythm — what we can call a Similarity–Attraction effect.

Let's break it down further:

- **Yang** energy moves **outward**, from the center to the edges

- **Yin** energy moves **inward**, from the edges to the center

This fundamental contrast explains their complementarity but also their tension. They are like inhaling and exhaling — they must follow one another in rhythm. If either becomes dominant or stuck, balance is lost, and life begins to deteriorate.

Yes, Pure Yin and Yang Do Exist

Another widespread misconception is that there is no such thing as pure Yin or pure Yang. But this is incorrect — especially in the context of energy practice.

- **Sunlight** is an example of **pure Yang**

- **Gravity** is an example of **pure Yin**

Both are powerful and fundamental to the structure of the universe. Just because something is Yin does not mean it is weak. Gravity is Yin, but we cannot say it is soft or passive — it is the very force that holds the physical universe together.

Five States of Yin–Yang

To understand real balance, we must also recognize that Yin and Yang can each be strong or weak, and that balance is a unique state of harmony between them. These are the five key conditions:

State	Description
Weak Yin	Insufficient inward force, leads to overactivity, dryness, or instability
Strong Yin	Excess inward force, leads to stagnation, cold, or depression
Weak Yang	Deficient outward force, causes fatigue, poor circulation, or lack of clarity
Strong Yang	Excess outward force, leads to restlessness, heat, or aggression
Balanced Yin–Yang	Dynamic equilibrium between forces, supporting health, harmony, and spiritual growth

Understanding these five conditions is essential for internal cultivation, because they lay the foundation for working with the Five Phases (Wu Xing 五行) — the next layer of Daoist energetic understanding.

The Ancient Yin–Yang Diagram

Far older than the modern Taiji symbol is a simpler diagram: a circle divided evenly into black and white halves, without dots or curving lines. This older symbol emphasizes the actual separation and polarity of Yin and Yang forces.

In its center is often placed a small empty circle, representing Wu Ji (無極) — the Limitless, the undivided, the state before duality. From this *Wu Ji* arises *Taiji* - Yin and Yang. This cycle represents the unfolding of existence and the path of return in Daoist internal alchemy.

Yin–Yang in Practice

For the Daoist practitioner, Yin–Yang is not just a theory — it is a map of the body, the mind, and the cosmos. It teaches us how to recognize imbalance, how to guide Qi, how to regulate the Five Spirits, and ultimately, how to return to the state of One.

To apply this wisdom, we must abandon rigid formulas and observe carefully: When to rest (Yin), when to act (Yang), when to cultivate softness, and when to refine strength. In this way, Daoist cultivation becomes not a struggle, but a rhythm — like inhaling and exhaling, like night and day.

Balance is not static — it is dynamic. Yin and Yang do not cancel each other out. They dance.

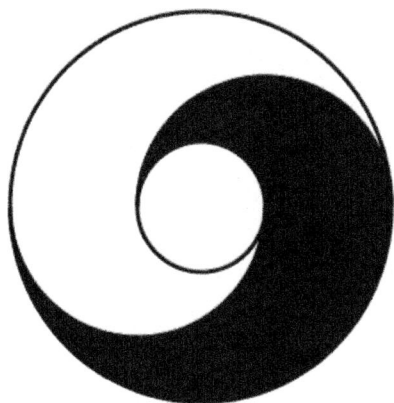

Five Yin–Yang States and Their Effects

State	Yin–Yang Relationship	Energy Behavior	Physical Effects	Mental / Emotional Effects
Weak Yin	Yin too low; Yang relatively excess	Insufficient inward, cooling, or anchoring force	Dryness, restlessness, poor sleep, overheating	Anxiety, scattered thoughts, emotional instability
Strong Yin	Yin excessive; Yang suppressed	Excess inward force, constriction, or accumulation	Cold limbs, stiffness, low metabolism, fatigue	Depression, emotional shutdown, dullness
Weak Yang	Yang too low; Yin relatively excess	Inadequate outward, warming, or expanding force	Coldness, weak digestion, low vitality, pale complexion	Apathy, lack of motivation, mental fog
Strong Yang	Yang excessive; Yin unable to balance	Excess outward, active, or dispersing force	Heat symptoms, inflammation, high blood pressure	Irritability, aggression, hyperactivity
Balanced Yin–Yang	Yin and Yang in dynamic harmony	Rhythmic alternation; Qi flows naturally	Vitality, adaptability, physical balance	Clarity, emotional stability, centered awareness

Every imbalance is an opportunity to restore harmony. Daoist practice teaches how to observe, recognize, and gently return to the center.

Wu Xing (五行)
The Five Phases of Dynamic Power

The concept of Wu Xing (五行) is one of the foundational principles of Daoist cosmology and cultivation. It is often mistranslated as "Five Elements," but this interpretation has led to widespread misunderstanding. The character 行 (*Xing*) does not mean "element" — it means *movement, process,* or *phase.*

In truth, Wu Xing refers to Five Dynamic Phases or Five Modes of Transformation. These are not static substances, like the classical Greek elements of water, earth, air, and fire. Instead, they are cyclical energy states — ways energy moves, transforms, nourishes, and interacts within both the Universe and the human body.

The Five Phases

Phase	Chinese	Energetic Nature
Water	水 (*Shuǐ*)	Strong Yin – descent, depth, storage
Wood	木 (*Mù*)	Arising Yang – growth, expansion
Fire	火 (*Huǒ*)	Strong Yang – ascent, radiance
Earth	土 (*Tǔ*)	Balanced – centralizing, stabilizing
Metal	金 (*Jīn*)	Arising Yin – contraction, condensation

These names — Water, Wood, Fire, Earth, Metal — are symbolic metaphors. They do not refer to physical substances. That is a common mistake. The names were chosen because each one expresses the energetic character of the phase it represents:

- **Water** flows downward and gathers — just like Yin

- **Wood** pushes upward and outward — like Yang beginning to rise

- **Fire** rises and spreads — the climax of Yang

- **Metal** contracts and condenses — the return of Yin

- **Earth** nourishes and stabilizes — the harmonizing center

Do not mistake the metaphor for the reality. These are not "things" — they are movements of Dao within the world and within yourself.

Wu Xing as Transformation

Wu Xing describes how energy:

- **Generates** (生) – one phase gives rise to another (e.g., Water → Wood)

- **Controls** (克) – one phase regulates another (e.g., Water controls Fire)

- **Draining / Diminishing** – one phase draining its source (e.g., Water diminishes Metal)

火
Fire

木
Wood
Tree

土
Earth

水
Water

金
Metal

- **Insults** – when the controlling relationship is reversed (e.g., Fire insulting Water)

These interrelationships are not rigid. They shift constantly based on the internal and external environment. Wu Xing is thus not a closed system — it is a living rhythm.

Wu Xing as Manifest Yin–Yang

Each Phase is also a manifestation of Yin–Yang dynamics in motion:

Phase	Yin–Yang Expression
Water	Strong Yin
Wood	Arising (nascent) Yang
Fire	Strong Yang
Metal	Arising (nascent) Yin
Earth	Balanced Yin and Yang

These are not absolute forces, but energy phases moving through the cosmic and human system. When properly understood and harmonized, they form the framework of balance in internal alchemy.

The Ancient Diagram: A Cross, Not a Star

While modern diagrams often use a five-pointed star to represent Wu Xing's controlling cycle, ancient Daoist sources depict the Five Phases in the form of a cross (十字) — not a star. This reflects the energetic tension and polar symmetry more clearly:

- Water opposite Fire

- Metal opposite Wood

- Earth at the center

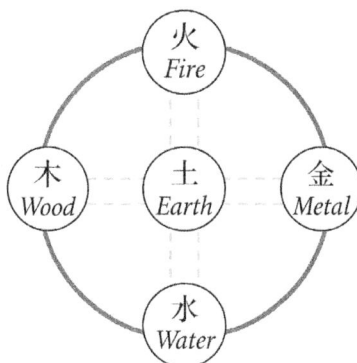

This cross structure is deeply connected with internal alchemy, where the practitioner uses these forces within the body to

45

harmonize, refine, and eventually transmute them into higher states of energy and spirit.

Applications of Wu Xing

Each phase has many correspondences — organs, seasons, emotions, directions, colors, spirits, and more. These correspondences are not arbitrary. They reflect how the macrocosm (the universe) and the microcosm (the body) are woven from the same patterns.

For example:

- Water (Kidneys) governs willpower and the season of winter

- Fire (Heart) governs spirit and joy, connected to summer

- And so on…

This is not just symbolic. In Daoist medicine, Dao Yin, Qigong, and Neidan, these correspondences help the practitioner understand how to balance and nourish internal energies, based on time, season, and inner condition.

Wu Xing is not about five things — it is about how Dao dances through cycles. To master the Phases is to move with the flow of Heaven and Earth.

Wu Xing in the Human Body

In Daoist medicine and internal cultivation, each of the Five Phases corresponds with specific organs, emotions, and energetic tendencies in the human body. These relationships are not arbitrary or invented. They were revealed through long observation, deep meditative insight, and direct communion with the Dao.

- **All Yin organs** (*Zang* 藏) are solid and have a storing function — thus they are energetically receptive and Yin.

- **All Yang organs** (*Fu* 腑) are hollow and have a releasing function — thus they are active and Yang in nature.

These correspondences were not made to create theoretical symmetry — they are grounded in real interactions between the human inner world and the living rhythms of the surrounding Universe.

Example: Energetic Connection of Organs and Emotions

- Excessive salt harms the Kidneys (Water phase), weakening their ability to regulate fluids — especially in winter (Water's season).

- Sudden fear (the emotion linked to Water) can disrupt Kidney energy so strongly that the paired Yang organ, the Bladder, may lose control — resulting in involuntary urination.

These are not symbolic observations. They reflect objective reality that can be confirmed in the body through practice, medicine, and meditation.

Four Cycles of Wu Xing Dynamics

Let's now examine the energetic cycles between the Five Phases. These cycles form the basis for both diagnostic understanding and practical cultivation.

1. Inter-Promoting Cycle (Generating / Nourishing Cycle 生)

Phase A	Promotes	Phase B
Wood	feeds	Fire
Fire	produces	Earth
Earth	strengthens	Metal
Metal	enriches	Water
Water	nourishes	Wood

This is the natural growth cycle — how one energy phase creates and supports the next. In the body, this reflects organ relationships, energy transfer, and life-sustaining flow.

2. Weakening Cycle (Draining / Diminishing)

Phase A	Weakens / Drains	Phase B
Wood	depletes	Water
Water	diminishes	Metal
Metal	exhausts	Earth
Earth	smothers	Fire
Fire	consumes	Wood

This cycle reflects exhaustion due to overuse — for instance, one phase draining its source, or itself becoming overactive and depleting the next.

3. Inter-Regulation Cycle (Overcoming / Restraining 克)

Phase A	Controls	Phase B
Wood	restrains	Earth
Earth	contains	Water
Water	dampens	Fire
Fire	melts	Metal
Metal	cuts	Wood

This is the natural controlling cycle — a healthy form of regulation. Each phase keeps another in check, preventing overgrowth or imbalance.

4. Counteracting Cycle (Reverse / Insult Cycle 侮)

Phase A	Harms / Insults	Phase B
Wood	dulls	Metal
Metal	depletes	Fire
Fire	evaporates	Water
Water	destabilizes	Earth
Earth	rots	Wood

This is an abnormal reversal — where a phase harms the one that is supposed to restrain it. This indicates a serious energetic disharmony, often caused by deficiency, emotional shock, or long-term imbalance.

True harmony is not achieved by maximizing one phase, but by nurturing all five in correct rhythm. Internal Alchemy depends on this.

Wu Xing Correspondences in the Human System

Phase	Zang (Yin Organ)	Fu (Yang Organ)	Emotion (Qing)	Season	Direction	Color	Sense	Tissue	Spirit (Shen)
Wood	Liver (肝)	Gallbladder (膽)	Anger (怒)	Spring	East	Green	Eyes	Tendons	Hun (魂) — Ethereal Soul
Fire	Heart (心)	Small Intestine (小腸)	Excessive Joy (喜)	Summer	South	Red	Tongue	Vessels	Shen (神) — Conscious Spirit
Earth	Spleen (脾)	Stomach (胃)	Worry / Overthinking (思)	Late Summer	Center	Yellow	Mouth	Flesh	Yi (意) — Intellect / Intention
Metal	Lungs (肺)	Large Intestine (大腸)	Grief / Sadness (悲)	Autumn	West	White	Nose	Skin	Po (魄) — Corporeal Soul
Water	Kidneys (腎)	Bladder (膀胱)	Fear (恐)	Winter	North	Black / Dark Blue	Ears	Bones	Zhi (志) — Willpower

Notes on Use in Cultivation

- These correspondences allow practitioners to harmonize their practice with seasons, emotional tendencies, and internal conditions.

- In Neidan, awareness of these interrelations helps guide refinement of the Five Spirits, transformation of essence–energy–spirit (Jing–Qi–Shen), and movement toward restoring balance in the Zang–Fu system.

- In Qigong and Dao Yin, movements, breath, and intent are often tailored to strengthen or release specific organs or emotional patterns based on these relationships.

"Heaven, Earth, and Human align through the Five Phases. Cultivation begins when their rhythms return to one."

Basic

Philosophy

Dao (道): The Source and the Way

Today, the term Dao (道) is widely used across many fields and often associated with broad ideas such as flow, balance, or nature. "Daoist philosophy" is increasingly popular, yet what is often presented as Dao is far removed from the depth, subtlety, and sacred meaning carried within the Daoist tradition itself. To truly approach the meaning of Dao, one must return to the original teachings that have been passed down for thousands of years — teachings rooted not in theory, but in the aspiration to directly comprehend the truth of existence.

Dao as the Source of All Things

In Daoism, Dao is not just a path or idea — it is the Primordial Source, the origin of all that exists and does not exist. It is the Original Reality that gives rise to time and space, yet is beyond both. It cannot be grasped by ordinary concepts, because it precedes form, category, and name.

Laozi's *Dao De Jing* (道德經), the foundational Daoist classic, opens with this profound line:

道可道，非常道
The Dao that can be spoken is not the constant Dao.

This first line already reveals the heart of the matter: Dao is not something that can be named, described, or captured through language. It is not a "way" in the ordinary sense — it is not a path that can be walked with the feet or mapped with the intellect. It is the Mysterious, the Nameless, the Self-Thusness/Naturalness (自然).

Yet although Dao transcends all forms, it also pervades all things. It is both beyond the world and within it. It animates the stars and moves through the veins of a tree. It breathes through every

53

human being, though most are unaware of it. Dao is the law behind all other laws, the subtle unfolding of Heaven and Earth, and the pattern behind all patterns.

Why the Mind Cannot Grasp Dao

Because Dao is limitless, it cannot be fully comprehended by the ordinary mind, which is formed and shaped by limited experiences. From childhood, our awareness is directed outward. We are taught to interpret life through layers of concepts, emotions, goals, and cultural conditioning. This forms the Post-Celestial self — a collection of acquired patterns that filters our perception of the world.

The result is a narrowing of consciousness. We become caught in opinions, attachments, and personal narratives. The mind becomes a mirror clouded with dust.

But according to Daoism, our Original Spirit (Yuan Shen) remains pure beneath these layers. The goal of the Daoist path is to clear away the Post-Celestial conditioning and return to the clarity of our Original Consciousness. In doing so, we become able to perceive Dao directly — not as a concept, but as a living presence.

From Post-Celestial to Pre-Celestial Awareness

Aspect	Post-Celestial (後天 – Hòu Tiān)	Pre-Celestial (先天 – Xiān Tiān)
Source of Awareness	Conditioned mind, shaped by external input	Original Spirit (*Yuan Shen*), pure awareness
Perception	Through learned filters and social identity	Direct, clear, non-dual perception
Mind	Fragmented, reactive, ego-centered	Still, spacious, selfless
Energy (Qi)	Acquired Qi, unstable, easily drained	Yuan Qi, rooted and resilient
Spirit (Shen)	Scattered, distracted, influenced by emotions	Unified, luminous, aligned with Dao
Intent (Yi)	Driven by goals, desire, fear	Centered in presence and clarity
Relationship to Dao	Separated, conceptual, speculative	Merged, embodied, experiential
Path of Cultivation	Cleansing, harmonizing, restructuring of body and mind	Inner union, silent realization, return to Original Nature
Symbolic Movement	Outward (from self to world)	Inward (from world to Source)
Daoist Practice Aim	Reverse the flow — from branches (effects) to the root (cause)	Return to the undivided — unity of Human, Heaven, and Earth

Cultivation is not about gaining something new — it's about returning to what you've always been, before conditioning began.

Dao as the Way

Dao also means Path — the Way of cultivation that leads back to the Source. This is another core meaning of the character 道: it represents not just the Origin, but also the method, process, and journey through which we return to it.

In Daoist practice, Dao is:

- The **goal** (realization of the Truth)

- The **path** (method of cultivation)

- The **process** (actual transformation that occurs along the way)

This inseparability of principle, path, and outcome is a defining characteristic of Daoist thought. Dao is what we seek, the means by which we seek it, and the very seeking itself. Because of this, Daoism resists rigid doctrines or static definitions. It teaches us to remain flexible, to adapt, and to trust direct experience over fixed belief.

The Symbolism of the Character 道

The character for **Dao** is rich with meaning.

- The **left part** (辶) means *walking*, or *movement with pauses* — symbolizing the personal journey of cultivation.

- The **right part** (首) means *head*, and includes deeper symbols:

    - The **upper portion** symbolizes the **United Universe**, with two dots representing **Yin and Yang** — the dynamic duality of existence.

- The **lower portion** (自) symbolizes the **self**, divided into three sectors. These represent the **Three Treasures**:

  - **Jing** (Essence)

  - **Qi** (Energy)

  - **Shen** (Spirit)

Above this is a vertical line representing the **central channel (Zhong Mai)** — the pathway that connects Heaven and Earth within the human being. When the **Three Treasures** are refined and united, and the internal channels opened, the spirit becomes aligned with the Universe. **The One is realized**. In this moment, the separation between self and cosmos dissolves — and Dao becomes self-evident.

This entire process is symbolically encoded within the structure of the character 道.

Symbolic Structure of the Character 道 (Dao)

Component	Chinese	Literal Meaning	Daoist Symbolic Meaning
Left Radical	辶	"Walk" / "Movement with pauses"	Represents the *Path*, the journey of cultivation, and the unfolding of the Way through time
Right Upper Part	丷 + 一	Two dots above a horizontal line	Symbolizes Yin and Yang within the United Universe — duality within Oneness
Right Lower Part	自	"Self"	Represents the *Three Treasures* (Jing, Qi, Shen) and the *Three Dantians* in the body
Central Vertical Line	(in 自)	Connecting line through "self"	Symbolizes the Zhong Mai (central channel) — integration and alignment of Heaven and Earth within the human
Combined Right Part	首	"Head"	Implies that the entire universe is within the mind; perception is shaped by consciousness
Whole Character 道	Dao	"The Way" / "The Path"	Reflects both the Source (Dao as Origin) and the Journey (Dao as Method) toward realization

Interpretive Notes:

- Three Sectors in 自 (Self): Symbolize Jing, Qi, Shen, or Lower, Middle, Upper Dantian — layers of human energy and awareness.

- Central Line: Represents the opening of the central channel, essential in Neidan for merging Heaven and Earth within.

- Dao as a Whole: Expresses the union of the path we walk, the principle behind all existence, and the transformational process through which we return to the Source.

From Being to Non-Being

The Daoist path is not about accumulating knowledge or reaching outward — it is about returning inward, from the branches to the root, from Being to Non-Being. Through correct practice, the separation between "self" and "Nature" is revealed to be a Post-Celestial illusion. True cultivation leads to the integration of the three external realms (Heaven, Earth, and Human) with the three internal Treasures (Jing, Qi, Shen). This culminates in the awakening of Original Nature, and the becoming of a True Immortal (*Zhen Xian* 真仙).

On Translation, Tradition, and the Role of the Teacher

Translating the *Dao De Jing* — or any Daoist classic — is extremely difficult. Classical Chinese lacks grammar structures familiar to modern languages: no tense, gender, articles, or conjunctions. One phrase can contain layers of meaning, and the deeper significance often lies between the words.

As a result, every translation reflects the translator's understanding, not just of language, but of Dao itself. This is why a living teacher is indispensable. Only someone who has experienced the path directly can clarify the theory and guide others in its practical application.

Moreover, one must recognize that Daoism is not a single monolithic system. There are many Daoist schools, each with its own lineage, terminology, and emphasis. What is correct in one school may not apply in another. For example, the Zheng Yi tradition and the Quan Zhen Jiao school have different practices and philosophical bases. Even within lineages descending from Lü Dongbin, such as those of Wang Chongyang and Zhang Boduan, there are significant differences in how and when inner practices are introduced.

Confusing one school's teachings for universal truths leads to misunderstanding — and often, to arrogance. True Daoism respects diversity within unity and understands that each method points toward the same Source, but speaks differently according to time, context, and the level of the student.

Do not mistake the finger for the moon. The words are not the Truth — they only point the way.

Daoist Cosmological Unfolding

Daoist cosmology offers a profound framework for understanding how the undivided source (Dao) gives rise to the world of multiplicity — both in the external universe and the internal human microcosm. Across Daoist traditions, two primary models of cosmological unfolding are commonly used. While they differ in language and emphasis, they are not contradictory. One model presents a structural vision of how the universe unfolds; the other reveals how practitioners return to the origin through internal cultivation.

Model One: Structured Cosmological Sequence

As seen in: Taijitu Shuo 太極圖說, *Xiuzhen Tu* 修真圖

This model lays out a cosmological sequence beginning in absolute stillness and culminating in manifest diversity. It maps both the macrocosmic world and the inner human structure.

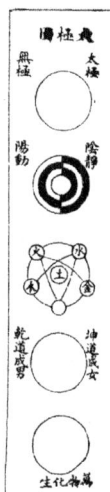

Daoist Cosmological Unfolding

Stage	Chinese Term	Meaning	Role in Cosmology
Dao	道	The Way; Supreme Source beyond all categories	The ineffable origin of all existence; beyond being and non-being
Limitless	無極 (*Wu Ji*)	Limitless; undivided, stillness, void	Pure potential; state before polarity or manifestation
Supreme Ultimate	太極 (*Taiji*)	Supreme Ultimate; unified origin of Yin and Yang	First differentiation; source of movement and polarity
Yin and Yang	陰陽	Complementary opposites: receptive & active, inward & outward	Dynamic duality that gives rise to cycles, rhythms, and transformation
Five Phases	五行 (*Wu Xing*)	Wood, Fire, Earth, Metal, Water	Qualitative transformations within nature and body; patterns of change
Ten Thousand Things	萬物	All phenomena, beings, and manifestations	The manifest world in all its diversity and multiplicity

Interpretation:

- **Wu Ji (無極)** is pure, undivided stillness — the source of all manifestation.

- **Taiji (太極)** is not only the origin of Yin and Yang, but also their totality and balance. As Zhou Dunyi states: "陰陽一太極也" — Yin and Yang are one Taiji.

- Yin and Yang, in turn, interact and transform into the Five Phases, which cycle through all changes to produce the Ten Thousand Things.

In the Xiuzhen Tu (修真圖) — a visual map of internal cultivation — Taiji is not labeled in words, but symbolically represented. A Taiji spiral or circle appears near the top of the head, above the Niwan Palace (泥丸宮), symbolizing the Original Spirit (元神). This placement reflects the unity and clarity of consciousness before duality arises. Yin and Yang, often represented by Fire and Water (or the trigrams Li and Kan), are shown below — not separate from Taiji, but as its manifest expression.

Note:
Since the diagram does not explicitly label this upper symbol as "Taiji (太極)," some traditions interpret it as a symbol of Wuji (無極) — the state of pre-differentiated potential. Others regard it as Taiji, representing the dynamic unity of Yin and Yang before they split. In either case, it marks the central axis of inner cultivation: the return to the Original Spirit (元神) and the realization of unity beyond duality. Whether it is seen as Wuji or Taiji depends on whether the practitioner is contemplating the source before movement or the harmonized field of Yin–Yang within stillness.

Thus, this model illustrates how Dao unfolds into creation, and how the human body mirrors that same cosmological unfolding — while also pointing the way to return.

Model Two: Numerical Cosmological Sequence

As seen in: Dao De Jing Chapter 42; interpreted in Neidan (Inner Alchemy)

This model uses symbolic numerology to describe how unity gives rise to multiplicity — and, in alchemical practice, how that process is reversed.

道生一，一生二，二生三，三生萬物

Dao gives birth to One. One gives birth to Two. Two gives birth to Three. Three gives birth to the Ten Thousand Things.

Stage	Manifestation	Interpretation
Dao	—	The nameless origin
One (一)	Wu Ji	Undivided unity
Two (二)	Yin–Yang	Polarity born from movement within unity
Three (三)	San Cai (三才)	Yin, Yang, and their harmonizing interaction (Zhong Qi); also seen as Heaven–Earth–Human — the cosmic triad
Ten Thousand Things	萬物	The manifested world

In Neidan (內丹):

- Liu Yiming explains: the One is Hunran Yi Qi, the undivided primal energy; Two is Yin and Yang; Three is the Zhōng Qì (中氣), their harmonized Qi of Yin and Yang — the Qi of unity: "一者，混然一氣也。二者，陰陽也。三者，中氣也，陰陽和合之氣也。"

- Three is also traditionally interpreted as the Three Powers (三才): Heaven (天), Earth (地), and Human (人) — the cosmic trinity of existence. Human beings serve as the bridge between Heaven and Earth, and in Daoist practice, cultivation occurs by aligning the three.

- Wang Mu emphasizes that this numerical sequence maps the logic of internal alchemy: the practitioner reverses the flow from multiplicity to unity.

In practical Neidan, this means refining the Three Treasures (精 Jing, 氣 Qi, 神 Shen), harmonizing Heaven–Earth–Human within the body, and returning to the One — and ultimately to Dao.

Thus, this model focuses not on external structure, but on internal reversal — the path of returning to Dao.

Comparison and Integration

Aspect	Structured Sequence	Numerical Sequence
Source Text	*Taijitu Shuo*, *Xiuzhen Tu*	*Dao De Jing* Chapter 42, Neidan commentaries
Focus	Macrocosmic structure and mapping	Inner transformation and reversal
Role of Taiji	Origin and unity of Yin and Yang	Implied as One or harmonizing Two
Role of Yin–Yang	Emerge from Taiji, and cycle	The "Two" born from unity
Ternary Integration	Implied through transformations	Explicit: Yin + Yang + Zhong Qi, or Heaven–Earth–Human
Application	Cosmology, metaphysics, internal body maps	Neidan, spiritual cultivation, internal alchemy

These two models are complementary perspectives. One shows how Dao unfolds; the other shows how the practitioner returns to Dao. The Xiuzhen Tu embodies both: it maps the cosmological descent, but is structured for the practitioner to reverse that descent through practice.

And central to both models is Taiji — not merely a point between Wu Ji and Yin–Yang, but the very field in which unity becomes duality, and duality returns to unity.

Dao is the source.
Wu Ji is the potential.
Taiji is the first breath.
Yin and Yang are the flow.
The Five Phases are transformation.
The Ten Thousand Things are experience.
But return is the movement of the Dao.

Daoist Cosmology and the Big Bang

While Daoist cosmology is rooted in spiritual and philosophical insight, it can be intriguingly compared with modern scientific models such as the Big Bang theory. Though the language and aims differ, both systems describe the emergence of complexity from an undivided origin.

Daoist Stage	Chinese Term	Big Bang Analogy	Explanation
Dao	道	Pre-Big Bang Singularity / the Unknown	The source beyond comprehension, before time and space — undefinable and formless
Wu Ji (Limitless)	無極	Singularity (zero entropy, undivided state)	Pure potential with no differentiation, no motion — comparable to a singularity
Taiji (Supreme Ultimate)	太極	Initial fluctuation or symmetry breaking	First stirring, initiating separation, movement, and pattern
Yin–Yang (Polarity)	陰陽	Emergence of fundamental forces	Duality and interaction — like matter–antimatter, gravity–expansion
Five Phases	五行	Formation of subatomic particles and atoms	Energy takes on characteristics, differentiating into modes of transformation
Ten Thousand Things	萬物	Galaxies, planets, life, consciousness	All phenomena — complex systems, matter, and beings

Both models describe a progression from undivided unity to diverse manifestation. In Neidan (Inner Alchemy), this sequence is reversed through practice: the practitioner refines body and mind to return to the origin — echoing the scientific search for a unified theory behind all forces and phenomena.

Some Parallels

1. Undivided Origin → Differentiation

- **Dao / Wu Ji** = the **initial undifferentiated state**

- In science, this is before Planck time, where physics breaks down

- Both point to a singular non-dual origin that is not directly observable

2. Taiji = First Movement

- The Taiji moment corresponds symbolically to the moment the singularity "breaks", releasing energy and space-time

- It's the origin of polarity — like the birth of the fundamental forces

3. Yin–Yang = Fundamental Dynamics

- Just as Yin and Yang are cyclical, interdependent, and self-balancing,

- So too are gravity vs expansion, matter vs antimatter, entropy vs structure

4. Five Phases = Qualitative Differentiation

- The Five Phases (Wu Xing) are not elements but modes of transformation

- They can loosely reflect how energy condenses into particles, and into states that interact

5. Return Through Reversal

- Neidan practice reverses this flow — returning from multiplicity to unity

- This could be likened to the idea of gravitational collapse or the theoretical Big Crunch, or more metaphorically, to the scientific quest to trace all back to the Unified Field

Caution: This is Not a One-to-One Match

- **Daoism is ontological and experiential** — about lived unity and return

- **Science is descriptive and empirical** — about measuring external phenomena

Still, both recognize that everything comes from an undivided beginning, and both show a sequence of emergent complexity.

In the Language of the Dao De Jing:

道生一，一生二，二生三，三生萬物
Dao gives birth to One. One gives birth to Two. Two gives birth to Three. Three gives birth to the Ten Thousand Things.

Compare this with:

Quantum fluctuation $\rightarrow$ symmetry breaking $\rightarrow$ forces $\rightarrow$ matter $\rightarrow$ galaxies $\rightarrow$ life

Both describe a cascade of unfolding, where One becomes Many, and point to the possibility of returning to the One — in science through unification of forces, in Daoism through spiritual cultivation.

Centers and
Channels

Centers and Channels in the Human Energy System

According to the Daoist tradition, in addition to the physical organs and systems, the human being also possesses a subtle energy body. This includes a network of channels through which the Life Force (Qi) circulates and energy centers that store, accumulate, refine, and transform this Qi.

The human energy system is complex, multilayered, and dynamic. In this section, we will focus on a general overview to form a foundational understanding suitable for entering the Daoist path of inner cultivation.

The Three Dantians

In Daoist alchemy, the body contains three primary energy centers known as the Dantians (丹田) — literally "Elixir Fields." These are sometimes metaphorically called cauldrons, reflecting their transformational function. The three centers are:

- **Lower Dantian** (下丹田)

- **Middle Dantian** (中丹田)

- **Upper Dantian** (上丹田)

While some people consider Dantians simply as storage batteries for energy, this is only a surface-level understanding. Each Dantian corresponds to a different layer of human existence, and each manifests the Dao in its own unique way. Their proper

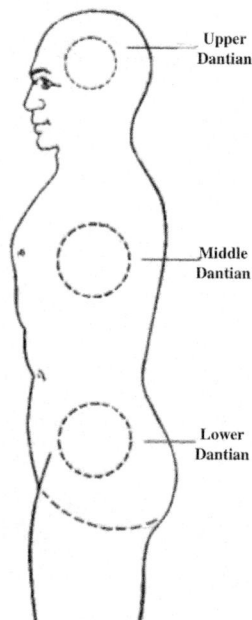

development and transformation form the very heart of Neidan (內丹, Inner Alchemy).

Lower Dantian — The Foundation

- **Location:** In the lower abdomen, behind and below the navel, at the depth of the Qihai (氣海) point. The back door of this center is the Mingmen (命門) — the "Gate of Life," located on the lower back, opposite the navel.

- **Function:** The Lower Dantian is the root of physical vitality, sexual energy, and the storage of Essence (Jing, 精). It supports the body's physiological functions and acts as the foundation for the upper centers. A weak or unstructured Lower Dantian can lead to health issues and block progress in internal practice.

- **Transformation:** Through the stage called "Building the Foundation" (築基), students learn to seal energy leaks — a process known as "Repairing Without Leakage" (修無漏) — and to transform the ordinary Dantian into a true alchemical furnace. This stage is often referred to as "Stabilizing the Furnace and Setting the Cauldron" (穩爐立鼎).

Just as you cannot melt metal in a kitchen pot, you cannot refine the elixir of immortality in an unprepared Dantian.

Once this center is stabilized and energetically awakened, practitioners can begin the alchemical merging of Yin and Yang, creating the Inner Elixir (Neidan) to nourish the Original Spirit (Yuan Shen, 元神) and awaken the True Nature (Zhen Xing, 真性).

Middle Dantian — The Heart-Mind Gate

- **Location:** Inside the chest, slightly above the solar plexus, aligned with the physical heart.

- **Function:** This center governs the emotional, personal, and moral dimension of life. It is linked with Heart-Mind (Xin 心) and emotional vitality — not physical strength, but the strength of will, character, and feeling.

- **Role in Cultivation:** The Middle Dantian is central to the Cultivation of Original Nature (Xing Gong, 性功) and Virtue (De, 德). Through this center, one opens the Gate to Heaven, allowing entry into the spiritual realm and resonance with the Primordial Spirit.

Cultivating this center helps purify emotions, dissolve egoic desires, and align the emotional heart with the Cosmic Heart / Heart of Heaven — a key step in the unfolding of true spiritual perception.

Upper Dantian — The Home of the Original Spirit

- **Location:** Deep within the cranial cavity, encompassing the pineal gland, pituitary gland, hypothalamus, and related brain structures.

- **Function:** This center governs consciousness, intuition, and spiritual vision. It plays a crucial role in awakening the Yuan Shen (元神) — the Original Spirit — and developing Original Wisdom (元慧).

- **Structure:** The Upper Dantian contains nine internal palaces, each associated with different spiritual functions. These are studied only at advanced levels, as work with this center requires subtle perception, stability, and precision.

Activation of the Upper Dantian leads to inner illumination, expanded perception, and a direct understanding of the deeper patterns of the Universe.

This is the center of true awakening and the domain of Dao-realization. It is not only the "residence" of the Original Spirit but the gateway to its awakening and return.

Clarification: Dantians vs. Chakras

Although both Dantians and Chakras refer to energetic centers, they are not the same system. Dantians are alchemical fields with specific transformational and cosmological roles, whereas Chakras are associated with a different spiritual map and philosophical base (primarily from Indian traditions). The locations, functions, and methods of cultivation differ significantly.

Energy Channels in the Human Body

In modern times, many people have heard of energy channels —
often described as invisible pathways through which Qi (Life
Force) circulates, just as blood flows through arteries and veins.
This idea has become especially widespread due to the global
expansion of acupuncture, a system that traces its origins to the
ancient Daoist tradition.

While popular knowledge often touches only the surface,
traditional Daoist cultivation presents a much more profound and
intricate understanding of the body's energetic structure — one
that integrates anatomy, cosmology, and spiritual transformation.

Meridian System Overview

According to classical Chinese medicine and Daoist internal
practice, the energetic system is composed of:

- **12 Standard Meridians (Regular Channels)**

- **8 Extraordinary Meridians (Curious or Special Channels)**

The 12 standard meridians are responsible for the routine
circulation of Qi throughout the body. They are bilateral and are
divided into Yin and Yang channels.

Yin Meridians of the Arm	**Lung, Heart, Pericardium**
Yang Meridians of the Arm	Large Intestine, Small Intestine, Triple Burner
Yin Meridians of the Leg	Spleen, Kidney, Liver
Yang Meridians of the Leg	Stomach, Bladder, Gallbladder

These are often referred to as **"rivers"** of Qi. They interconnect and circulate Qi throughout the body, forming the basis of many external practices such as acupuncture and Tuina.

The Eight Extraordinary Meridians

The extraordinary meridians are considered reservoirs or lakes of Qi. They help regulate and supplement the standard meridians, storing excess energy and providing deeper, stabilizing functions. When the primary channels are deficient, they draw energy from these extraordinary vessels. If those are also depleted, the system turns to the Dantian, especially the Lower Dantian, which is why keeping it well-filled is vital.

Extraordinary Meridians
Conception Vessel (Ren Mai)
Governing Vessel (Du Mai)
Central Channel (Zhong Mai)
Girdle Vessel (Dai Mai)
Yin Linking Vessel (Yin Wei Mai)
Yang Linking Vessel (Yang Wei Mai)
Yin Heel Vessel (Yin Qiao Mai)
Yang Heel Vessel (Yang Qiao Mai)

Among these, three channels are especially central to inner alchemy:

Governing Vessel (Du Mai) – Sea of Yang Meridians

- **Origin:** Begins deep inside the Lower Dantian, emerges at the perineum, and travels up the spine.

- **Pathway:** Ascends the midline of the sacrum, spine, neck, and head; one branch enters the brain, another surfaces at Baihui (百會) at the crown and descends along the face to the upper lip.

- **Function:** Governs Yang meridians, helps regulate Guardian Qi (Wei Qi), and is connected to immunity and protection.

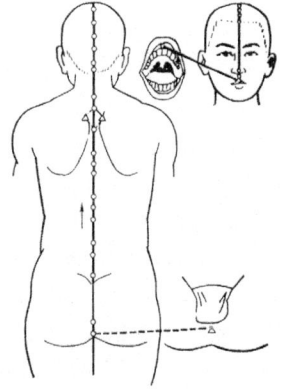

Conception Vessel (Ren Mai) – Sea of Yin Meridians

- **Pathway:** Starts at the Huiyin (會陰) point and ascends the front midline of the body to the lower lip.

- **Function:** Governs the Yin meridians, nourishes the body's Yin, and is linked with deep nourishment, receptivity, and growth.

- **Small Heavenly Circle (小周天):** When the Governing (Du Mai) and Conception (Ren Mai)

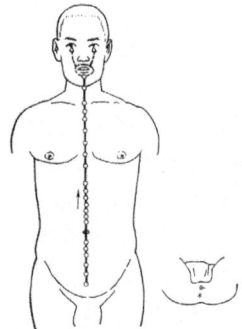

are connected via the tip of the tongue touching the upper palate, the Small Heavenly Circulation is activated. This forms the first major energetic orbit in Neidan.

Note: The Small Heavenly Circle is more than the popularized "microcosmic orbit." In the Daoist tradition, its correct activation requires proper instruction, deep meditative absorption, and understanding of spiritual transformation. Without spiritual clarity, technical repetition is insufficient.

Central Channel (Zhong Mai) – Axis of Alchemical Unity

Bai Hui

- **Pathway:** Begins at the Huiyin point and rises within the body, piercing through all three Dantians, and ending at Baihui at the crown.

- **Function:** Called the Central Channel, Middle Channel, or Penetrating Vessel, this is the axis of the subtle body and the inner ladder for the ascent of spirit.

In advanced cultivation:

- This is the channel through which the spirit can consciously leave the body.

- It is used in the practice of "Proper Death" (正死), in which a practitioner unites Shen (Spirit) and Qi and guides them toward transcendence.

Hui Yin

Zhong Mai supports the vertical alignment of Heaven–Earth–Human within the body. It integrates the Three Dantians and allows the realization of the Body of Light (光身) — a state of inner illumination and Celestial Immortality (天仙).

Because of its profound function, this channel plays a central role in Neidan alchemy, though its methods are often transmitted only within oral lineages.

The Three Treasures (三宝)

Jing (Essence) · Qi (Life Force) · Shen (Spirit)

The theory of the Three Treasures (San Bao, 三宝) is one of the most essential foundations of Daoist cultivation. It is at the heart of both basic health practices and advanced Inner Alchemy (Neidan 內丹). A correct understanding of the Three Treasures is vital, as the entire process of self-cultivation — from physical development to spiritual transformation — involves their regulation, refinement, and unification.

Jing (精) — Essence

- **Translation:** Essence · Life Essence · Seed · Root Energy

- **Location:** Stored primarily in the Lower Dantian and kidneys

- **Associated with:** Hormonal system, glands, DNA / RNA, stem cells, reproductive capacity

Jing refers to the most fundamental energy of the physical body. It is the substance of vitality, the deep root of life, and determines the body's structure and longevity. In traditional texts, Jing is often compared to the seed of a plant — the foundation from which all life grows.

There are two types of Jing:

1. Original Jing (Yuan Jing, 元精)

Also called Pre-Heaven Jing, this is the innate essence inherited from your parents. It forms the blueprint of your body and is limited in quantity. This type of Jing is gradually consumed throughout life through aging, stress, excessive sexual activity, illness, or trauma. When Original Jing is depleted, life comes to an end.

Original Jing is not easily replenished. It requires special methods of Neidan to restore, refine, and protect it.

2. Post-Heaven Jing

This is the Jing derived from food, water, and air — created and transformed through digestion and respiration. Although it can be replenished more easily, the quality of this Jing depends on lifestyle, diet, and environment.

Not all Jing is equal: "Living" Jing (from fresh, vital food and clean air) still retains its Qi, while "dead" Jing lacks vitality and contributes less to true health.

Why Jing Matters

- It determines your physical strength, reproductive capacity, and lifespan.

- It is the foundation for cultivating Qi and Shen — without sufficient Jing, deeper cultivation is impossible.

- Jing is the substance which, when refined, becomes Qi, and later, Shen. This is the first stage of inner transformation.

Regulation and Cultivation of Jing

At the initial stages, working with Jing means:

- Strengthening the physical body (flexibility, breath, posture)

- Reducing leakage of Jing (stress management, lifestyle regulation)

- Proper diet and rest

- Sealing and storing (固精) through internal practices

In advanced stages, Neidan practice involves refining Post-Heaven Jing to strengthen Yuan Jing, and eventually transforming it into Qi to fuel the alchemical process.

"When Jing is full, it transforms into Qi; when Qi is full, it transforms into Shen; when Shen is stabilized and returned, one attains unity with the Dao."

Qi (氣) — Life Force Energy

The Second Treasure of Daoist Cultivation

Qi (氣) is the vital force that animates and sustains life. It is the second of the Three Treasures and plays a central role in all Daoist cultivation. Without Qi, no physical, energetic, or spiritual function can be maintained. It is Qi that makes the heart beat, the blood circulate, the organs function, and even the mind perceive and think. In Daoist understanding, Qi is not just energy; it is the connecting thread between Heaven, Earth, and Humanity — the bridge between Jing (Essence) and Shen (Spirit).

Pre-Heaven and Post-Heaven Qi

Like Jing, Qi is divided into Pre-Heaven Qi and Post-Heaven Qi. The Original or Pre-Heaven Qi (Yuan Qi, 元氣) is received from our parents at the moment of conception — a direct result of the union of Yin and Yang through the merging of sperm and egg. This energy forms the foundation of our vitality and is responsible for our growth and development through early life. Yuan Qi is stored mainly in the Lower Dantian and kidneys, and although it continues to support life into adulthood, the natural ability to increase it ceases around the age of 14.

When this Original Qi is exhausted, life comes to an end. That is why protecting and refining Yuan Qi is a core goal in Neidan (Internal Alchemy). Ordinary people continuously consume their Yuan Qi throughout life, but through internal practice, it is possible to nourish, replenish, and even regenerate this essential treasure.

After birth, the body begins to rely on Post-Heaven Qi, which is drawn from the air we breathe, the food we eat, and the energetic quality of the environment. This type of Qi circulates constantly through the body and is closely connected to everyday physiological function. The Lower Dantian is the main center for refining Post-Heaven Qi, where it can be transformed into other energies or used to supplement Jing. The Middle Dantian is responsible for further refining Qi into a more subtle form that can support emotional clarity and spiritual insight.

Transformations and Types of Qi

Within the body, Qi and Jing can be transformed into one another depending on internal conditions or through deliberate practice. The body may convert Qi into Jing when needed to support the physical essence. At the same time, cultivated Jing can be refined into Qi to fuel spiritual development.

There are many classifications of Qi in Daoist medicine and cultivation, but two important types are:

- **Wei Qi (Protective Qi)** – a defensive layer of Qi that circulates near the skin's surface and protects the body from external harm or pathogens.

- **Ying Qi (Nourishing Qi)** – the Qi that flows through the internal channels, nourishing the organs and regulating internal functions.

Both of these types circulate along the meridians and form part of the energetic basis of health. However, deeper Daoist cultivation also involves working with higher expressions of Qi — especially in the process of spiritual refinement.

Types of External Qi

In the Daoist tradition, Qi is not limited to the energy circulating within the human body. It also exists externally, in nature and in the universe, in a range of subtle forms and qualities. Daoist texts and teachings identify a clear hierarchy of external Qi, reflecting the way Dao unfolds into breath and energy, from the undivided cosmic source to the refined presence of Spirit in the world.

Understanding these levels of Qi helps practitioners recognize how to interact with energy at different stages of refinement—from absorbing the living energy of nature to cultivating the sacred breath that nourishes the Spirit. In this chapter, we'll explore five principal types of external Qi and how they appear in Daoist thought and alchemical practice.

Qi of Nature (自然之氣)

Qi of Nature is the most basic and accessible form of external Qi. It is the life force naturally present in forests, mountains, rivers, fresh air, and sunlight. This energy is ambient, formless, and untamed. It can be felt after a rainfall, at sunrise in the mountains, or deep in a forest far from human interference.

In Daoist cultivation, this Qi is often the first to be collected, using breath, posture, and intention. It replenishes the body, supports physical health, and restores harmony to the organ systems. Methods such as Cai Qi (gathering energy) train the practitioner to absorb this energy and refine it in the Lower Dantian.

Though coarse compared to higher forms, Qi of Nature is alive, and proper interaction with it is an essential part of Daoist training.

Qi of Light (光氣)

Qi of Light is a more refined and subtle form of energy. As one advances in practice and inner sensitivity, Qi begins to appear not only as sensation but also as radiance—a subtle light, often perceived internally as colored glow or translucent movement.

Qi of Light is no longer simply collected from nature but also generated and perceived through focused meditation, quiet breath, and the awakening of inner stillness. It connects physical energy to Spirit and plays a crucial role in transforming Qi into Shen.

Many Daoist texts refer to this quality of energy in the context of visions, dreams, and states of heightened consciousness. It often appears as a sign of the refinement process—when external Qi becomes internal and luminous.

Ling Qi (靈氣) — Numinous Manifest Qi

At the highest level of external Qi is Ling Qi, often translated as numinous or sacred Qi. It is not merely refined—it is spiritualized. Ling Qi is Qi that has become clear, luminous, and alive with Dao. It is found in sacred mountains, in the breath of awakened sages, and in advanced states of internal alchemy.

Daoist scriptures speak of Ling Qi as the energy through which all sacred life emerges. In 雲笈七籤 (Yún Jí Qī Qiān) says:

人稟靈氣以生
"Humans are animated by the vital and numinous Qi"

Ling Qi is not physical or visible, but it is manifest. It appears as sacred presence, deep clarity, or the radiant stillness felt in temples or when meeting a true teacher. In Neidan, when Qi becomes Ling, it can nourish Yuan Shen (Original Spirit), catalyze inner transformation, and open the gate to transcendence. When humans are animated by Ling Qi, the Yuan Shen may emerge from concealment — the True Spirit awakens not merely through existence, but through resonance with the numinous. This type of Qi leads to the formation of the Light Body. Ling Qi is the final expression of Qi before it returns to the Dao, or perhaps the first breath of the Dao entering the world.

Yuan Qi (元氣) — Original Qi

From Hunran Yi Qi, movement begins. The first breath of the universe emerges: Yuan Qi, often translated as Original Qi or Primal Qi. It is the first differentiation from stillness—the subtle One from which Two and Three emerge.

This is reflected in the Dao De Jing, Chapter 42:

道生一，一生二，二生三，三生萬物
"The Dao gives birth to One. One gives birth to Two. Two gives birth to Three. Three gives birth to the Ten Thousand Things."

Yuan Qi is the source of Heaven and Earth, and it is also the root of our own vitality. At the human level, it is the Pre-Heaven essence inherited from our parents. It is stored in the kidneys and Lower Dantian and can be preserved and refined through correct Daoist practice.

Unlike Qi of Nature, Yuan Qi is not replenished by food or breath, but through deep inner stillness and alchemical refinement.

Hunran Yi Qi (渾然一氣) — Undivided Primordial Qi

Long before the existence of light or form, Daoist cosmology speaks of Hunran Yi Qi, the "single, undivided Qi." It refers to the original state of the universe before any division into Yin and Yang —when all things were immersed in silent, complete unity.

The *Zhuang Zi* describes this condition beautifully:

渾然一氣，未分陰陽
"There was a single undivided Qi, not yet separated into Yin and Yang."

Hunran Yi Qi is the "breath" of the Dao before it stirs, before there is differentiation, when the universe remains in a state of perfect internal unity. It is not yet manifest. It is pure potential. While not used directly in physical or energetic practices, its philosophical role is foundational: it is the ground from which all Qi arises.

The Path of Refinement

These five types of Qi do not stand apart, but rather represent stages along a path—from Dao to breath to Spirit:

- **Hunran Yi Qi** is the Dao's undivided presence.

- **Yuan Qi** is the first movement.

- **Ling Qi** is sacred manifestation—the Spirit of Dao appearing in form.

- **Qi of Light** is radiant, refined energy.

- **Qi of Nature** is the raw breath of the living world.

The practitioner gradually learns to absorb, transform, and transcend each stage. As coarse Qi is refined, it becomes luminous. As light deepens, it becomes Ling. When Ling Qi is cultivated and unified with Shen, the body and mind can return to Dao.

Levels of External Qi

Name	Chinese	Meaning	Manifestation	Role in Cultivation
Hunran Yi Qi	渾然一氣	Undivided Primordial Qi	Pre-manifest stillness, pure unity	Earliest Qi of Dao before Yin–Yang; contemplative root of return
Yuan Qi	元氣	Original Qi	Subtle movement from stillness	Root of life and alchemy; stored in kidneys and Dantian
Ling Qi	靈氣	Numinous, sacred Qi	Spiritual presence, awakened clarity	Nourishes Yuan Shen; catalyst for transformation and realization
Qi of Light	光氣	Radiant, refined energy	Perceived as internal luminosity	Bridges Qi and Shen; develops inner clarity and subtle sensitivity
Qi of Nature	自然之氣	Vital energy of the environment	Fresh, ambient, unshaped natural energy	Supports health and grounding; used in early-stage energy gathering

Zhen Qi (真氣) – True Qi in Daoist Cultivation

In the Daoist tradition, 真氣 (*Zhen Qi*), or True Qi, holds a central role in the process of internal refinement. Yet it is often misunderstood. Unlike other types of Qi such as Yuan Qi (Original Qi), Ling Qi (Numinous Qi), or Qi of Nature, Zhen Qi is not a separate category of Qi with a distinct source or identity. Instead, it is a qualitative designation — it tells us what Qi has become through proper cultivation.

What Is Zhen Qi?

Zhen Qi refers to Qi that has been purified, balanced, and aligned with the Dao. It is Qi that has passed through essential transformations: it flows smoothly, in harmony with Yin and Yang, and is no longer scattered, turbid, or bound by egoic tension. It is the kind of Qi that naturally supports health, clarity, inner stability, and most importantly, alchemical transformation.

In this sense, Zhen Qi is a state of Qi, not a substance. It may emerge from Post-Heaven Qi (such as the Qi of breath and food) or from Pre-Heaven Qi (such as Yuan Qi), but it becomes "true" only when properly cultivated. This involves harmonizing the body, regulating breath, refining intention, and purifying Shen.

It is said in classical Neidan teachings:

「精化為氣，氣化為神，神還虛無。」
"Essence transforms into Qi, Qi transforms into Spirit, Spirit returns to Emptiness."

Here, it is the Zhen Qi that acts as the bridge between Jing and Shen. Ordinary Qi cannot carry out this transformation. Only when Qi becomes true — Zhen — can it serve as the foundation for internal alchemy.

Zhen Qi and the Other Forms of Qi

To understand Zhen Qi clearly, it helps to see how it relates to other key forms of Qi in Daoist thought:

Qi Type	Description	Relation to Zhen Qi
Hunran Yi Qi	混然一氣 – The Undivided Breath of the Dao, beyond Yin and Yang, beyond time.	Zhen Qi cannot "become" Hunran Yi Qi; rather, Zhen Qi must become *still and refined* enough to resonate with it.
Yuan Qi	元氣 – Original Qi, inherited from the Dao before birth.	Zhen Qi can be cultivated from Yuan Qi by harmonizing and refining it.
Ling Qi	靈氣 – Numinous Qi; manifest presence of Spirit.	When Zhen Qi is elevated and integrated with Shen, it may transform into Ling Qi.
Qi of Light	光氣 – Radiant Qi; refined and visible as subtle luminosity.	Zhen Qi may appear as Qi of Light when concentrated and aligned in spiritual practice.
Qi of Nature	自然之氣 – Ambient Qi from the environment.	Can be refined into Zhen Qi through correct Qi work, absorption, and internal harmony.

Thus, Zhen Qi is not a "higher" or "lower" form, but a refined and true state that other Qi types may attain through correct cultivation. It is a crucial milestone in the process of transforming Jing into Shen and ultimately returning to Dao.

Zhen Qi and Hunran Yi Qi

It is important not to confuse Zhen Qi with Hunran Yi Qi (混然一氣), the primordial, undifferentiated breath of the Dao itself. While Zhen Qi arises within duality — shaped through practice, balance, and intention — Hunran Yi Qi lies beyond all opposites. It is not formed, transformed, or corrected. It is the spontaneous, whole, unborn Qi from which all things arise.

Therefore, Zhen Qi does not return to Hunran Yi Qi in the sense of being merged or reabsorbed. Rather, when Zhen Qi becomes perfectly balanced, and Spirit returns to Emptiness, the practitioner may begin to resonate with Hunran Yi Qi. It may be reflected through stillness, or glimpsed in meditative absorption, but it is not a result of transformation. It simply is.

The Role of Zhen Qi in Cultivation

Zhen Qi plays a pivotal role in Daoist Neidan (Inner Alchemy). It is the bridge between the body's vitality and the Spirit's awakening. The refining of Qi into Zhen Qi marks the turning point where physical life-force begins to take on spiritual luminosity.

In this stage:

- The body's vitality becomes unified.

- Energy flows harmoniously through the channels.

- The Central Channel (Zhong Mai) begins to stabilize.

- The Lower Dantian becomes an Elixir Field (丹田) in truth.

With Zhen Qi circulating, the Small Heavenly Cycle (Xiao Zhou Tian) becomes more than a Qi practice — it becomes a vehicle of spiritual refinement.

Zhen Qi is not something a person "has"; it is something they become aligned with. It reflects the truthfulness of practice, the purity of intention, and the refinement of inner states. When Zhen Qi arises, it means you are no longer pushing Qi — you are cultivating Dao through Qi.

Only when Jing, Qi, and Shen are in harmony, and Qi becomes Zhen, can the Gate of All Marvelous-Mysterious open.

What Is 正气 (Zhèng Qì)?

正气 is typically translated as "Upright Qi," "Righteous Qi," or "Correct Qi." In Daoist and classical Chinese medicine contexts, it carries a variety of meanings depending on the layer of interpretation:

Classical Chinese Medicine (TCM) Meaning

In traditional Chinese medicine, Zhèng Qì is:

- The totality of the body's protective Qi (卫气), nourishing Qi (营气), and deeper constitutional vitality.

- It defends against external pathogens, maintains balance, and preserves health.

- It is not just Wei Qi, but includes both defensive and constitutional strength — a dynamic, living field of protection and inner balance.

《黄帝内经》："正气存内，邪不可干。"
Huángdì Nèijīng: *"When Zheng Qi is stored within, pathogenic Qi cannot invade."*

In this view, Zhèng Qì is associated with immunity, uprightness, and energetic integrity.

Philosophical and Spiritual Meaning

In Daoist cultivation, Zhèng Qì takes on a more moral, energetic, and spiritual tone:

- It is the Qi that aligns with Dao, flowing correctly, harmoniously, and without distortion.

- It reflects inner alignment, clarity of intention, integrity, and virtue (De, 德).

- In Neidan, Zheng Qi may be the result of successfully refined Qi that is in harmony with Heaven and Earth, Yin and Yang, and the Original Nature.

Some classical Daoist texts even use Zhèng Qì as a synonym for the force of the Dao within the human body — the upright channeling of the universal order.

Zhèng Qì (正气) vs. Zhēn Qì (真气)

These two terms are sometimes confused, so let's contrast them clearly:

Term	Chinese	Meaning
正气	Upright Qi	Qi that is upright, righteous, health-promoting, in harmony with Dao and moral integrity
真气	True Qi	Refined, balanced Qi — the authentic, real Qi formed through inner cultivation (Neidan)

They overlap in quality — both refer to Qi that is balanced, aligned, refined — but differ in emphasis:

- Zheng Qi emphasizes alignment with correctness and health (externally and internally).

- Zhen Qi emphasizes purity and authenticity — Qi that is free of distortion, whether physical, emotional, or spiritual.

Comparison with Other Types of Qi

Type of Qi	Chinese	Nature	Relation to Daoist Cultivation
Hunran Yi Qi	混然一气	Undivided, pre-cosmic unity — Breath of Dao	Beyond time and space; the original undivided oneness
Yuan Qi	元气	Original Pre-Heaven Qi	Root of life, inherited essence, stored in the Dantian
Ling Qi	灵气	Sacred, numinous, spiritual Qi	Catalyzes Yuan Shen, awakens spiritual clarity
Zhen Qi	真气	True, authentic Qi — refined and balanced	Result of successful Neidan stages; flows through transformed channels
Zheng Qi	正气	Upright, righteous Qi — aligned with Dao	Protects, regulates, and aligns both physical and moral-spiritual balance
Qi of Light	光气	Radiant Qi, luminous in nature	Seen in celestial harmonization and subtle alchemical transformation
Qi of Nature	自然之气	Expressed Qi of wind, trees, air, etc.	Entry-level cultivation — collected and refined from the environment

- Zhèng Qì is a marker of integrity. It is not only a health concept but a moral and energetic alignment.

- In medical terms, Zheng Qi is resistance and vitality.

- In Daoist terms, it is the Qi of a harmonious life, a channel for De (Virtue), and a shield of purity.

- While Zhen Qi (真气) may describe a stage of refinement, Zheng Qi (正气) reflects the direction and correctness of that refinement.

Five Types of Qi and Daoist Cosmological Unfolding

Daoist cosmology describes the process through which the Dao, the unmanifest source of all, gives rise to the multiplicity of existence. The same sequence is mirrored within human beings during internal alchemy (Neidan). Each stage of cosmological unfolding corresponds to a particular form or quality of Qi, from the most formless and absolute to the most differentiated and embodied.

Here is the correlation:

Stage of Unfolding	Cosmic Phase	Type of Qi	Explanation
Dao (道)	The Unnameable, Source of all things	— *(Beyond Qi)*	The Dao itself is not Qi, but the origin of Qi. It is absolute, unborn, unmanifest.
Wu Ji (無極)	Limitless; undivided stillness	Hunran Yi Qi (混然一氣)	The Undivided Qi of the Dao, a total unity without polarity. It is the primordial breath before Yin–Yang arise — the Breath of the Dao itself.
Tai Ji (太極)	Supreme Ultimate; origin of Yin and Yang	Yuan Qi (元氣)	As movement arises within stillness, the first stirring is Yuan Qi — Original Qi, pure potential, the beginning of dynamic differentiation.
Yin–Yang (陰陽)	Emergence of polarity	Ling Qi (靈氣)	Where Yin and Yang differentiate yet remain dynamically united, Ling Qi appears — a sacred, manifest Qi capable of interacting with consciousness.

Three (Heaven, Earth, Human)	Dynamic ternary — harmonized interaction of polarity	Qi of Light (光氣)	When Yin and Yang harmonize in movement (San), Qi becomes perceptible as Light, radiance of Spirit, present in celestial alignments and luminous Qi.
Five Phases → Ten Thousand Things	All manifest phenomena	Qi of Nature (自然之氣)	The expressed, environmental Qi in all things. This is the Qi of wind, water, earth, trees — the differentiated breath of life in the world.

Understanding the Relationship

These types of Qi do not merely exist in separation. They form a spectrum, from the most subtle and undivided (Hunran Yi Qi) to the most tangible and diverse (Qi of Nature). Cultivation moves in reverse — we start with the Qi of Nature and refine it back toward the Dao.

This corresponds with the reversal of the cosmological sequence in Neidan:

Qi of Nature → Qi of Light → Ling Qi → Yuan Qi → Hunran Yi Qi → Return to Dao

- **Qi of Nature** is gathered from breath, food, and environment.

- **Qi of Light** emerges through refinement and opening of perception.

- **Ling Qi** awakens spiritual presence and deepens Shen.

- **Yuan Qi** is accessed through inner stillness and activation of Pre-Heaven channels.

- **Hunran Yi Qi** is not generated — it is encountered when all else is dissolved.

Cosmological Model and Internal Practice

Cosmology Stage	Inner Cultivation	Qi Type in Practice
Dao	Non-dual realization, final merging with Source	— (Transcends Qi)
Wu Ji	Meditation, stillness, Original Emptiness	Hunran Yi Qi — glimpsed in great tranquility
Tai Ji	Awakening of internal unity, breath refinement	Yuan Qi — accessed in Dantian and Zhong Mai
Yin–Yang	Balancing energies, harmonizing Spirit and Qi	Ling Qi — experienced in Shen resonance
Three (Heaven, Earth, Human)	Synchronization with cosmic forces	Qi of Light — celestial attunement
Ten Thousand Things	Grounded presence, health, cultivation of Virtue	Qi of Nature — environmental absorption

Each form of Qi reflects a layer of existence, both cosmically and internally. Zhen Qi (真氣), as discussed earlier, is not a distinct form but a **quality** of Qi that may arise at any stage — when that Qi becomes refined, balanced, and aligned with Dao.

Thus, cultivation becomes a journey:

- From Nature to Origin,

- From divided to whole,

- From movement to stillness,

- And from Qi to Dao.

Shen – The Third Treasure

Shen (神), often translated as "Spirit" or
"Soul," is the third of the Three Treasures in
Daoist cultivation, alongside Jing and Qi. It is
Shen that gives us intelligence, awareness, self-
reflection, and the capacity for spiritual
growth. Like the other two treasures, Shen
exists in two aspects: **Yuan Shen (元神)**, the
Original or Primordial Spirit, and **Shi Shen (识
神)**, the Conscious Spirit or Spirit of
Recognition.

The Original Spirit is our eternal, divine essence. It carries
profound wisdom and remains unchanged across incarnations. In
contrast, the Conscious Spirit forms after birth under the influence
of culture, environment, and personal experiences. It shapes our
personality, thoughts, emotions, and the way we perceive the
world.

Yuan Shen resides in the Upper Dantian, while the door of Shi
Shen is located in the heart. Still, both are present throughout the
entire body; they cannot be confined to a single point. In Daoist
alchemy, restoring the clarity and presence of Yuan Shen is
essential, for only through it can one comprehend the Original
Nature and attain immortality.

Shi Shen is further composed of two components: **Hun (魂)** and
Po (魄). According to classical teaching, a human being has **three
Hun souls** and **seven Po souls**. The Hun souls represent the Yang
aspect of the Conscious Spirit—light, intelligent, and spiritual.
They reside in the Liver and are associated with arising Yang in
the Five Phases system. The Po souls, by contrast, represent the
Yin side—dense, emotional, and instinctual. They reside in the
Lungs and are linked to arising Yin.

Because the Po souls outnumber the Hun, our natural inclination leans toward desire, emotion, and earth-bound tendencies. One of the core goals of Inner Alchemy is to refine the Po and nourish the Hun, gradually turning the Conscious Spirit into a pure vessel for Yuan Shen.

At death, both Yuan Shen and Shi Shen leave the body. The Hun is said to dissolve into Heaven, and the Po into Earth. The Shi Shen, formed during one life, dissipates, while the Yuan Shen carries the karmic imprints to the next incarnation. Therefore, Daoist alchemy aims to bring about the **merging of Shi Shen with Yuan Shen** before death, achieving what is known as True Immortality.

To prepare for this merging, the Conscious Spirit must be purified. It must be emptied of emotional agitation, delusions, and attachments formed through Post-Heaven conditioning. Only in a state of sincerity and inner stillness can true knowledge and higher forms of Qi be received. A common teaching is: "Empty your mind and open your heart; enter a state of sincerity."

Before incarnation, the Yuan Shen prepares to enter a new body, while the Shi Shen has not yet been formed. In the womb, the Shi Shen is pure and reflective—it faces inward, gazing toward the Yuan Shen. At birth, the Conscious Spirit turns outward to engage with the sensory world. This is necessary for functioning in the world, but it also marks the beginning of karmic influence and the loss of inner clarity.

The practice of **Purification of the Mind** is a return to that original state of clarity. It means removing all the conditioning and influences that have polluted the Shi Shen, returning it to the state of a blank slate. When this is achieved, the Yuan Shen can once again become the Master, and the Conscious Spirit the Guest.

It's important to understand that Shi Shen is not something to be destroyed. It is your individuality and the vehicle through which your Original Nature can be expressed. What must be "killed" or transformed is not the Spirit itself, but the delusions and ego attachments that obscure it. This is what is sometimes referred to as "killing the ego."

When the Shi Shen becomes still and inward-facing, it can once again perceive the Yuan Shen. This meeting leads to a gradual merging. The result is a return to the condition before birth—a fusion of Pure Individuality with the Original Spirit. At this level, the practitioner becomes fully realized yet retains unique personal expression. That is why true Masters do not appear identical. Though they are united in essence, they each embody the Dao in a personal and spontaneous way.

Among the Three Treasures, Shen holds the highest position, though all three must be cultivated and regulated in harmony. Regulation of Jing involves the body—maintaining structural alignment, vitality, and clarity of physical presence. Regulation of Qi involves the breath and energy—balancing and refining circulation. Regulation of Shen involves clearing the mind of confusion and emotional disturbance, restoring stillness and clarity.

These Three Regulations form the basis of Daoist cultivation. Just as a musical instrument must be tuned before it can play, the body, energy, and spirit must be harmonized before any advanced work in Inner Alchemy can begin. Only when the Three Treasures are in order can one proceed to the deeper phases of spiritual transformation.

Xing and Ming – Dual Cultivation

There are thousands of methods in Qigong, Neigong, and Neidan. Yet all of them can ultimately be classified into two primary categories: **Ming Gong (命功)** and **Xing Gong (性功)**.

Ming Gong refers to the **Cultivation of Life**, where "Life" signifies the Life Force—Qi. This includes all practices that regulate the physical body, breathing, and internal energy. These methods train the Jing–Qi–Shen system and lay the physiological and energetic foundation for more advanced transformation.

Xing Gong, on the other hand, means the **Cultivation of Inner Nature** or **Original Nature (Xing)**. This area of practice relates to the Heart–Mind (Xin), consciousness, soul, and Spirit. It is the spiritual branch of cultivation, aimed at refining and awakening one's Original Nature, restoring sincerity, and returning to the Dao.

Both aspects are essential in the Daoist path. In fact, true cultivation must integrate both. This is expressed in the well-known phrase:
"Xìng mìng shuāng xiū" (性命双修) — "Dual Cultivation of Xing and Ming."

If a practitioner works only with one aspect—whether it is only the body and Qi (Ming), or only the spirit and morality (Xing)—the practice remains imbalanced. Such an imbalance will eventually become a barrier to deeper realization. Without harmony between Xing and Ming, one cannot attune to the Original State of the Universe on all levels of being.

The ancient Masters offered a clear image to help us understand their relationship: **Xing is the light; Ming is the oil.**
The flame of the spirit cannot shine without the sustaining oil of life. The oil by itself is useless unless it is lit. Only when light and oil are combined can illumination occur. This is the very principle of dual cultivation.

For teaching purposes, Xing and Ming may be presented as separate domains, but in actual practice, they are never truly apart. It is only for beginners and clarity of understanding that they are explained as two complementary forces to be unified.

Many great patriarchs—such as Lu Dongbin, Wang Chongyang, and Qiu Chuji—emphasized that real cultivation must begin with Xing Gong. Spiritual growth begins not with energetic force but with sincerity of heart, clarity of mind, and purification of inner nature. Xing Gong is the section that opens the path toward spiritual realization. And the first and most important step in Xing Gong is the Cultivation of Virtue (De).

Without working on the heart and mind, a person who practices only Qigong may become healthy, energized, and even powerful —but not necessarily wise. The ego may grow stronger, and the practitioner may develop attachment to their progress, their abilities, or their identity as a "spiritual person." This path leads away from Dao, not toward it.

Why does this happen? The answer is simple: cultivating only the body, Qi, and ordinary consciousness is not yet spiritual work. Good health and abundant energy do not, by themselves, lead to awakening. It is a common misconception that vitality automatically brings virtue or realization. But without inner refinement, without ethical clarity and selflessness, the path remains worldly.

That is why ancient Masters taught that the cultivation of Virtue must come first. Before you refine Qi or stabilize Spirit, you must purify the Heart. Let go of ignorance. Uproot desire. Develop humility, compassion, sincerity, and courage. These are not minor teachings—they are the core of the Dao.

Only when the Heart is upright and the Spirit luminous can the Qi flow in harmony and the Jing be preserved. When the foundations of both Ming Gong and Xing Gong are cultivated together, the path becomes stable and clear. One rises steadily toward Dao not only with strength, but with light.

Building the Foundation

In Daoist Cultivation, nothing is more essential than Building the Foundation. Without it, no higher achievement is possible. Just as a house must be built on solid ground, your spiritual and energetic cultivation must rest on a firm and well-prepared base. Skipping or neglecting this phase often leads to stagnation, imbalance, or even harm.

Many people, driven by enthusiasm or curiosity, attempt to jump straight into advanced Inner Alchemy practices. But without the proper groundwork, such practices cannot yield lasting results. True cultivation is a long path, and success comes only to those who respect the stages and honor the sequence.

Body Foundation

The physical body is the starting point of all real cultivation. If the body is weak or unhealthy, the mind will be restless, the energy unstable, and the inner transformation difficult. A strong, flexible, and harmonized body not only supports energetic development—it becomes the vessel through which Spirit can manifest.

One of the most effective ways to begin is through traditional martial arts such as **Taichi (Taiji)** or other styles of **Wushu**. These practices cultivate strength, balance, coordination, and sensitivity. They also train the practitioner to use the body as one integrated whole, which is vital for proper Qi circulation and mental focus.

Another profound method is the ancient art of **Dao Yin (導引)**. This system of stretching, breathing, and intention-guided movement helps to open the meridians, harmonize the organs, and settle the mind. When practiced correctly, it leads not only to improved health and structure, but also to inner awareness and clarity.

It is important to seek out traditional forms of these arts, rather than simplified or modernized versions designed primarily for relaxation or therapy. While gentle Qigong for health can be valuable—especially in cases of illness or recovery—those who are already healthy should focus on forms that build strength, resilience, and depth.

If traditional methods are unavailable, there are many other ways to prepare the body. Hiking, fitness routines, and even consistent walking can improve vitality and build discipline. What matters most is consistency, attention, and a spirit of refinement.

Relaxation – The Gateway to Flow

One of the most essential skills in Daoist Foundation training is **relaxation** (松, *sōng*). True relaxation is not limpness or laziness—it is the active release of unnecessary tension from the body, breath, and mind. Most people carry hidden stress in their muscles, joints, nervous system, and thoughts. This blocks energy, clouds awareness, and fragments the Spirit.

To build the right inner environment for cultivation, we must learn to let go—of muscular stiffness, of emotional tightness, of mental grasping. Relaxation must become a habit, a natural state of being. It begins with the body, but quickly extends to the breath, nervous system, and the subtle field of the Heart–Mind.

True *sōng* is relaxed yet alert, soft yet alive, open yet grounded. It is not a collapse, but a return to natural alignment. Only in this state can Qi flow freely, Shen become luminous, and the Elixir of transformation begin to form.

Building the Foundation is not a "beginner's phase" to be rushed through. It is a living practice that continues even at the highest levels. The deeper your foundation, the more stable your spiritual house will be. Whether you are training for health, longevity, or the great return to Dao, your first step is always the same: build the base, cultivate relaxation, and enter the path with humility.

Heart–Mind Foundation

The cultivation of the Heart–Mind is at the very core of the Daoist path. Known as **Xīnjìng (心静)**, it refers to the state of inner stillness, quietude, and clarity of awareness. This is not a superficial calm, but a deep and luminous tranquility of the spirit —free from disturbance, agitation, or emotional turbulence.

To establish this foundation, the heart-mind must first be cleansed of turbid energy, negative emotions, and scattered thoughts. The base for this work is Virtue Cultivation and Relaxation. Without these two elements, no method of Qigong, Neigong, or Neidan can reach its full potential. Every practice requires the ability to focus, remain present, and guide the spirit inward.

In the beginning, most people quickly discover that their mind does not easily obey. Attention jumps from one thought to another, emotions flare without cause, and restlessness takes hold. This condition is known in Daoist and Buddhist traditions as the Monkey Mind—wild, chaotic, difficult to tame.

But how can you build a spiritual foundation if your mind behaves like a monkey swinging from branch to branch? The answer lies in regular, sincere training. Though it may seem more difficult than physical discipline, cultivating the Heart–Mind is absolutely necessary. Without it, even the best techniques become empty repetition.

It is not enough to sit still, close the eyes, and call it meditation. The state of tranquility is not a state of dullness or stupidity. Many practitioners fall into this trap—sitting like a stone, without intention, inner work, or spiritual openness. They wait passively for something to happen, mistaking stillness for practice. But waiting is not Cultivation. The only result from this is the ability to wait longer.

True practice requires conscious presence and connection. When you enter a meditative posture, you should align body, energy, and mind with Nature. Become open to the vast field of Heaven and Earth. Let your Original Nature resonate with the Original Nature of the cosmos. This is the internal preparation for true Cultivation.

Stillness in Daoism does not mean lifeless stasis. It is dynamic potential—the fertile stillness that contains all movement. In the Daoist view, stillness holds motion, and motion returns to stillness. Tranquility is not limited to the meditation cushion. It must enter every part of your life—while walking, speaking, working, or resting. It should become your second nature.

This leads to another fundamental quality: **Naturalness**.

Daoist teachers often say, "Be Natural." But what does this really mean? Does it mean following every impulse, every desire? Certainly not. Many of our so-called "natural" tendencies arise not from the Original Nature, but from a corrupted body, restless mind, or unrefined emotions. If we blindly follow such impulses, we fall deeper into confusion.

Therefore, true Naturalness must be cultivated. It is not simply allowed to arise on its own. The path to authentic Naturalness lies through three gates: Virtue, Relaxation, and Tranquility.

- **Virtue Cultivation** cleanses the heart and opens sincerity.

- **Relaxation** harmonizes energy, calms the nervous system, and prepares the mind.

- **Tranquility** provides the space in which Naturalness can manifest—free of tension, ego, or distortion.

Because this work is subtle and easily misunderstood, it is essential to have a qualified Teacher. A true Teacher can see your condition more clearly than you can and guide your progress with precision and compassion. Many things that feel unnatural at first are, in fact, steps toward your true nature. And many things that feel comfortable are nothing but habits of confusion.

Students must learn to examine their inner impulses with honesty. A good practice is to ask oneself:

- "Will this help me improve myself?"

- "Does this serve my true development or only my ego?"

- "Is this leading me toward clarity, or toward indulgence?"

Answering these questions sincerely brings clarity. In time, your Heart–Mind becomes aligned with the rhythms of the Dao. You begin to sense what is appropriate, what is beneficial, what is real. You move in harmony with the seasons, feel the presence of Heaven and Earth, and **Naturalness becomes your true nature**.

This is the essence of the Heart–Mind Foundation. It is the gateway to everything that follows. Without it, the house of cultivation cannot stand. With it, you begin to awaken the light within.

Virtue Cultivation – Where Students Should Start

In modern times, many students of Daoist cultivation eagerly seek out Qigong exercises, Neigong sequences, or even advanced methods of Inner Alchemy—yet they often overlook the most essential foundation of all: Virtue Cultivation.

Without virtue, no method—no matter how ancient or refined—can bring lasting spiritual transformation. Virtue is not merely a moral principle or cultural ideal; it is the living foundation of the Daoist path. It is the soil in which all authentic practices must be rooted. Without this ground, no elixir can form, no Spirit can be stabilized, and no deep harmony with the Dao can be realized.

Yet what exactly is meant by "Virtue," and where should a student begin?

Daoist tradition offers direct and practical guidance. Two classical scriptures in particular provide valuable instruction:

- **Taishan Lao Jun Talks About the One Hundred Diseases**
  (太上老君说百病)

- **Taishan Lao Jun Glorifies the One Hundred Medicines**
  (老君崇百药)

These texts describe the moral and mental conditions that give rise to internal imbalances (called "diseases") and the corresponding spiritual and ethical remedies ("medicines") that can restore harmony.

Both texts are translated and explained in Book 2 of this series, offering students a reliable and accessible foundation for understanding Virtue Cultivation in the Daoist tradition. These scriptures illuminate how physical and spiritual well-being are inseparable from ethical behavior, clarity of mind, and sincere intention. When studying these texts, it is important to discuss them with a Teacher, as some passages require clarification and deeper context to be fully understood.

Four Levels of Virtue

Traditional Daoism describes Virtue in four ascending levels:

1. **Lack of Virtue**
   When a person behaves only according to external rules or social norms, without any internal reflection. The actions may appear appropriate, but they are shallow and lack true spiritual foundation.

2. **Ordinary or Lower Virtue**
   When a person performs good deeds or shows moral behavior, but secretly hopes for reward, recognition, or personal benefit in return.

3. **Great Virtue**
   When one acts with integrity and kindness spontaneously and selflessly, without any expectation. The person acts from sincerity, not for outcome.

4. **Supreme Virtue**
   When Virtue becomes the natural expression of one's being. One helps others freely, guides them to reduce their suffering, and shares the Teaching—not to gain anything, but because it is the Way.

At this highest level, Virtue is not performed—it flows naturally from the practitioner's Original Nature. It reflects the Dao itself: silent, giving, and without trace.

The Living Practice of Virtue

Virtue is not merely a code of ethics. It is the art of living in harmony with others, with Nature, and with Heaven and Earth. It must be demonstrated through action, speech, and thought. A Daoist practitioner should be honest, sincere, reliable, compassionate, and humble—not only within their family, but also in their interactions with all people, animals, and the natural world.

It is not enough to speak of ideals. Virtue must be embodied.

Still, Virtue is not always easy to define in daily life. The boundary between selfish desire and true necessity is often subtle. What appears selfless may be rooted in pride. What feels natural may actually arise from conditioned tendencies or emotional distortions.

This is why students must be honest with themselves. If they cannot discern clearly, they should ask their Teacher:

- "Is this truly helpful to my path?"

- "Is this coming from clarity or from ego?"

- "Am I moving toward wisdom, or toward indulgence?"

By asking these questions sincerely, you begin to cultivate Discriminating Wisdom—the ability to sense what is appropriate and aligned with the Dao in each situation.

The Mind of Virtue

Virtue cultivation is fundamentally about transforming the mind and heart. It involves developing several key mental qualities:

- **The Mind of Beneficence (仁心)** — goodwill and generosity toward all beings

- **The Mind of Compassion (慈心)** — empathy for the suffering of others and a desire to relieve it

- **The Mind of Moral Conduct (道心)** — a deep inner compass that follows harmony rather than impulse

Start simply. Begin with small acts of kindness, restraint, honesty, and clarity. These small steps create habits. Habits shape character. And over time, your nature becomes clear, sincere, and deeply connected to the flow of Heaven and Earth.

As your virtue deepens, you will become more sensitive to what feels right in the moment. You will begin to follow the natural unfolding of situations rather than your own preferences. This is the beginning of real wisdom.

Virtue as the True Beginning

The ancient Daoist masters knew: a person who practices energy work without virtue may grow powerful, but not wise. They may become imbalanced, prideful, or even dangerous. But a person who cultivates virtue—even with simple methods—will move steadily toward the Dao.

That is why Virtue is the true beginning of the Way. It is also its ongoing practice and ultimate fruit.

When the heart is sincere, the mind can become still. When the mind is clear, the energy can be refined. And when the energy is harmonized, the Spirit can awaken.

This is where the journey begins.

The Three Ways

In the Daoist tradition, different schools may emphasize different methods, lineages, or philosophical orientations. However, beyond these surface differences lies a more universal map of spiritual progress—**the Three Ways of self-cultivation**. Regardless of the school, path, or tradition, all Daoist practices can ultimately be understood through the framework of these Three Ways: **the Lower Way, the Middle Way, and the Great Way**.

These are not stages of superiority or hierarchy in a moral sense. Rather, they reflect **depths of engagement with spiritual cultivation**—each one suitable for different capacities, karmic conditions, and phases of personal development.

The Lower Way — The Way of Purity

The Lower Way, often referred to as the **Way of Purity**, is the most accessible and universal among the Three Ways. It can be followed by anyone, regardless of age, background, physical ability, or spiritual experience. Its foundation is ethical living, moral clarity, and sincerity of heart.

The key elements of this path include:

- **Living a simple and sincere life**, guided by moral principles (not to kill, steal, lie, or harm)

- **Cultivating virtuous qualities** such as compassion, forgiveness, kindness, courage, humility, and generosity

- **Avoiding thoughts, speech, and actions** that can bring harm to others, to oneself, or to Nature

- **Helping others**—humans, animals, or plants—with words and deeds whenever possible

- **Respecting and supporting all forms of life**, not just those close to you

In essence, the Lower Way is about aligning one's daily life with **natural goodness and moral clarity**, fostering peace in both the inner world and the outer world.

This path also includes certain **ritual practices and interactions with sacred spaces or Masters**. Visiting temples, participating in ceremonies, or receiving guidance from a Teacher can help cleanse the heart, redirect attention from worldly concerns, and open a subtle channel to the higher realms.

Despite being called the "Lower" Way, it should not be underestimated. In truth, **sincere ethical living is far more difficult than it appears**, especially when one begins to examine the unconscious patterns, emotional tendencies, and culturally conditioned responses that dominate most people's behavior.

Even with intelligence, education, or social success, a person can remain **in darkness about the deeper questions of life**. Questions such as "What is death?", "What continues after the body dies?", or "What is my true nature?" are often avoided, feared, or answered only through borrowed beliefs.

Most people live with a great many **assumptions** about life and death—assumptions not based on direct experience, but on external ideas. In Daoism, only that which has been personally realized has true value. **Belief is not knowing**. And so, while a person may seem upright and virtuous in worldly terms, they may still live in **obscuration** about the deeper reality.

Nevertheless, the Lower Way offers a **solid and beneficial path**. Anyone can begin it—no special talent or advanced training is required. What matters is **sincerity, consistency, and inner honesty**.

The Fruit of the Lower Way

A person who truly realizes the Lower Way becomes what we might call **a Sage or a Saint**—someone who lives a noble life in accordance with virtue, supports others, and brings light into the world.

However, in the Daoist view, **even a virtuous person who follows only this Way remains within the cycle of birth and death (samsara)**. That is because ethical conduct alone does not lead to liberation from reincarnation. It clears karma and builds the foundation for deeper paths, but does not by itself reveal the Original Nature or achieve union with Dao.

Still, the merit of this Way is profound. One who perfects this path **accumulates great blessings**, and in future lives, will naturally be drawn to more direct and effective methods of spiritual cultivation. This karmic momentum forms **the bridge** to the Middle Way and, eventually, the Great Way.

Thus, even though it is called the Lower Way, it is by no means inferior. It is **a necessary and powerful foundation**—and for many, the ideal starting point for walking the Dao.

The Middle Way

The Middle Way incorporates all the moral and ethical principles of the Lower Way but adds a more structured and intentional effort toward spiritual transformation. Those who walk the Middle Way place a greater value on spiritual development and intentionally devote more time and attention to personal cultivation. The practices found here serve to accelerate internal transformation beyond what ethical living alone can accomplish.

This Way is sometimes referred to as Religious, in the highest sense of the word—not merely belief in something external, but sincere reverence for the Dao and the use of ritual, symbolism, and devotion as powerful tools for inner transformation.

Ritual as Symbol and Transmission

The Middle Way includes a wide range of practices involving deities, visualizations, prayers, invocations, and ritual offerings. These practices are not superstitions, nor do they require blind faith. Rather, they are symbolic actions designed to connect the practitioner to higher principles—to remind, realign, and awaken.

Offerings such as food, incense, or sacred objects are given not to flatter divine beings, but to express gratitude and humility, and to foster the understanding that not all things are within human control. In doing so, the practitioner reduces egocentric thinking and becomes open to higher influence.

At a deeper level, ritual practices serve as reflections of inner transformation. For example:

- A prayer for compassion may awaken compassion within.

- An offering to a deity of wisdom may activate one's own latent wisdom.

- A ceremonial invocation may help the practitioner attune to the subtle realm beyond sensory perception.

In this way, external action becomes a gateway to inner alignment. Correctly understood, these forms are vehicles—not the final destination.

Understanding the Role of Deities

In Daoist tradition, deities are not gods in the Western sense, nor are they creators or rulers. They are manifestations of Dao—specific emanations of the Supreme Source with distinct qualities, functions, and characteristics. These forms serve as bridges between the formless Dao and the human mind, which needs form to grasp the formless.

Anthropomorphism—portraying divine aspects in humanlike form—was used as a skillful means to make these principles easier to access and relate to. One deity may represent boundless compassion, another inner stillness, another courage, another healing. Through working with these forms, practitioners can develop and awaken corresponding virtues within themselves.

太清
道德天尊

玉清
元始天尊

上清
靈寶天尊

But this method has a subtle danger. As soon as Dao is given a form, it is already limited and distorted, because the true Dao is beyond name and shape. As the Dao De Jing reminds us:

"The Dao that can be spoken is not the eternal Dao." (道可道，非常道)

Thus, if the practitioner becomes attached to the form and forgets the formless Source, they risk halting their development. This is like mistaking the finger pointing at the moon for the moon itself.

Potential Mistakes on the Middle Way

If practiced without understanding, the Middle Way can easily fall into ritualism or dogma. External forms may be preserved, but their inner meaning may be lost. Students may continue to chant, bow, or perform offerings without true intention, connection, or understanding. When this happens, the practice becomes hollow, and the transformative power is lost.

Additionally, students may become too attached to their chosen forms or deities and fail to move beyond the symbolic into the real. Daoist cultivation must always return the practitioner to their Original Nature, to the Dao itself—not stop at its reflection.

To avoid these pitfalls, it is essential to receive direct guidance from a qualified Teacher, who can explain the inner significance of rituals and correct misunderstandings.

Fruit and Limitation of the Middle Way

When practiced sincerely and correctly, the Middle Way can lead a practitioner beyond the cycle of reincarnation. It can clear karmic burdens, awaken inner clarity, and open the door to profound realization.

However, in most cases, it may not bring the practitioner to the final transformation—that is, the complete refining of body, energy, and spirit into the Fǎ Shēn (法身), or attainment of True Immortality (真仙). This is because the methods, while powerful, often work at a moderate or symbolic pace, and may not engage the full inner alchemical mechanisms needed for final realization.

Thus, while the Middle Way is a noble and transformative path, it is still a bridge, not the destination. Its name reflects this balance— it is neither mundane nor transcendent, but somewhere in between.

The Great Way

The Great Way is the most difficult to understand and practice, yet it offers the greatest possible result in spiritual development within a single lifetime. For centuries, the methods of this path were transmitted only to a small number of chosen and highly capable disciples, and only in recent times—when the so-called "Time of Expansion of the Way" (弘道之時) has arrived—have some Masters begun to teach its introductory levels more openly.

However, even today, the advanced stages of this Way remain reserved for those who demonstrate sincere aspiration to realize the Dao, a high level of cultivated Virtue (De, 德), and real accomplishment in foundational methods. Only when a practitioner has laid a strong base in moral conduct, inner clarity, and energetic refinement can they be entrusted with the deeper alchemical practices of the Great Way.

Beyond Form and Ritual

Unlike the Middle Way, which often utilizes rituals, visualizations, and deities to engage the practitioner's symbolic mind, the Great Way often bypasses these altogether. Though it fully includes the ethical principles of the Lower Way, it may partially or completely exclude religious methods, especially in advanced stages.

The goal of this Way is not symbolic transformation, but direct realization of Dao itself—without depending on forms, representations, or intermediaries. Because of this, the risk of attachment to methods and images is greatly reduced, and the practitioner is guided straight into the depth of the Original Source.

The Dao is not limited by form. Its nature is formless, timeless, and infinite. In this Way, practitioners work not to describe Dao, but to dissolve into it. And through this dissolution, a person can surpass the limitations of the ordinary mind and conceptual consciousness, entering into direct union with the Original State.

The Challenge of the Formless

This direct approach, while extremely powerful, is also extremely difficult. The human mind clings naturally to structure, definitions, and categories. It is trained from childhood to work with the visible and tangible, to rely on logic, and to move through life according to learned systems of meaning.

But Dao cannot be contained in a system. It cannot be reduced to symbols. The Supreme Truth must be realized as it is, without labels and without conceptual frames. That is why the Great Way requires a radical letting go—a deep inner silence in which all movement and all thought are stilled.

In this sense, the Great Way is not religious in the conventional sense. It has no dogma, no fixed icons, and no outward rituals. What it requires is immersion into deep Quietness and Tranquility (靜)—and from that, transformation from within.

Direct Inner Alchemy

Instead of external practices and actions in the forms of rituals, etc., which are typical for the Middle Way and aim to induce inner transformations, methods of the Great Way employ direct work with internal states and energy, developed through a process of immersion into deep Quietness and Tranquility. This allows the practitioner to achieve profound internal transformation of the body, energy, and consciousness at a much faster pace. Thus, a maximal result can be attained in a minimum period.

The maximal result here is understood as the complete refinement and merging of the Three Treasures—Jing (Essence), Qi (Life Force), and Shen (Spirit)—into one unified state. Through deep internal transformation, the practitioner eventually manifests the Truth Body (法身, Fǎshēn)—a condition in which one is both merged with Dao and still capable of expressing individuality in the world. It is a realization of Dao not merely as concept or philosophy, but as direct experience, in which form and formlessness are no longer separate.

This extraordinary achievement was clearly explained by Wang Chongyang, the founder of the Complete Reality (Quanzhen) School, in his *Fifteen Discourses Establishing the Teaching by Wang Chongyang* (*Wang Chongyang Chuangjiao Shiwulun* 王重陽創教十五論), especially in Discourse 14. There, he elaborates on the nature and signs of attaining the True Body, carefully distinguishing it from lesser attainments or conceptual understanding. He emphasizes that only through the complete internal realization of Dao can one be said to have returned to the Original and True.

This important treatise has been translated and accompanied by detailed commentary in Book 9 of this series, offering students direct access to Wang Chongyang's inner teaching and the lived wisdom of the Great Way.

In some rare cases, a Master who has completed this process of internal merging will, at the time of death, dissolve into Clear Light, leaving no physical remains behind. The appearance of rainbow light or luminous transformation may accompany their departure, marking the ultimate refinement of form into energy— a sign that nothing has been left undone in their return to the Source.

This is the path of Inner Alchemy (Neidan, 內丹)—a profound, secret, and highly demanding Way. While it is the most powerful and complete method of Daoist cultivation, it is also the most difficult, and not suited for everyone.

Suitability and Adaptation

The Great Way is reserved for those with exceptional capacity, great perseverance, and unwavering sincerity. For most people, the Middle Way offers a more accessible path. It combines moderate alchemical methods with symbolic and devotional practices and may be enough to liberate the practitioner from rebirth and bring clarity and peace.

Those with average abilities may integrate basic Neidan with supportive religious practices. Those with less capacity may focus on preparatory methods only: refining the body, building life force, and calming the mind—all of which lay the groundwork for future transformation.

Importantly, it is better to practice sincerely within one's own capacity than to imitate a higher method without the necessary foundation. As training progresses, the capacity of the practitioner may expand, and it is the responsibility of a qualified Teacher to guide them to the next level when the time is right.

In all cases, the choice of the correct path must come from wisdom, not ambition.

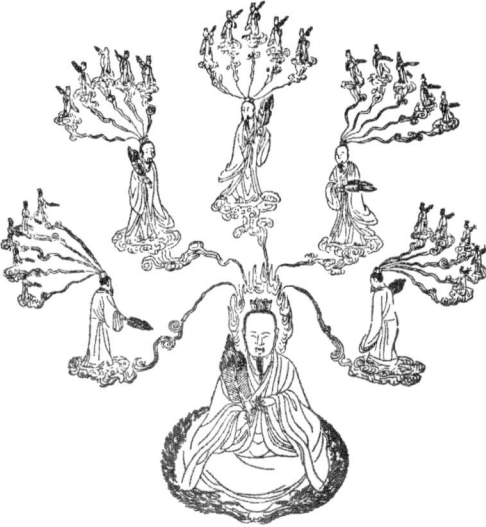

The Gate of All Marvelous-Mysterious

The stages of Daoist cultivation contain the following major steps:

1. Cultivating Essence (Jing) into Qi

2. Cultivating Qi into Spirit (Shen)

3. Cultivating Spirit to return to Emptiness

4. Cultivating Emptiness to merge with Dao

These are the foundational movements within the Daoist Way. However, they are not mechanical steps, but rather spiraling deepening stages of return. At the root of them all is one crucial transformation: Cultivating Intention (意念) to achieve the Mysterious (玄). This is the Gate through which all profound transformation arises.

This Mysterious (玄) is what Laozi called the "Mystery of Mysteries" — the "Gate of all Marvelous-Mysterious" (众妙之门). It is not a physical gate, nor a mental idea, but a state of being that marks the transition from the ordinary (post-Heaven) to the Origin (pre-Heaven), from scattered mind to unified spirit.

The Role of Intention and the Subtle

When we begin Qigong or meditative practices, we are often told to align posture, regulate breath, and quiet the mind. These are necessary—but insufficient on their own. One must cultivate subtle awareness of both inner and outer changes. This is where intention comes in: not a forceful will, but a quiet, sincere focus on the subtleties that lie beneath form.

At this stage, the practitioner begins to feel something deeper than ordinary Qi. At first, this may arise as **Qi of Nature (自然之氣)**—

the mist-like breath of wind, trees, and mountain air. Then, it may become **Qi of Light** (光氣)—a luminous and radiant presence felt within and around the body.

But if the practice matures, and one's heart-mind is tranquil and virtue is cultivated, one may touch **Ling Qi** (靈氣)—the visible manifestation of the spiritual Dao. Ling Qi reveals not only energy, but intelligence and responsiveness. It is the living breath of Dao's Presence.

Deeper still lies **Yuan Qi** (元氣)—the Original Qi, prefiguring form, gifted at conception, stored in the Lower Dantian, and awakened through deep inner stillness and sincerity. Yuan Qi is not moved by breath—it moves the breath. It is the basis of transformation in Neidan practice.

Entering the Gate of Mystery

And finally—when all these subtle layers harmonize, when intention becomes non-intention, when you feel something in your practice that cannot be named but cannot be denied—this is the approach to the Gate.

What lies beyond is not a substance, but a condition: the condition of **Hunran Yi Qi** (混然一氣)—the **Undivided Oneness Qi**.

Hunran Yi Qi is the primal breath before Yin and Yang. It is Qi before separation, before circulation. It does not flow—it pervades. It is the perfect blend of formless Presence and non-graspable Stillness. It is not a thing to be obtained, but a state to be remembered.

It is the breath of the Great Emptiness (太虛) — the Source of Sources. And although it may seem distant or abstract, the practitioner can recognize it by its qualities:

- It arises when one stops grasping.

- It deepens when virtue becomes natural.

- It opens when intention becomes silent sincerity.

What Happens at the Gate?

The Gate of All Marvelous-Mysterious is not a fixed place, nor is it reached through time. It is the condition in which subtle returns to Origin. It is the moment when the Qi cultivated dissolves into Hunran Yi Qi. The Spirit merges into Stillness. The practitioner begins to see the Dao not as a goal—but as the ever-present field in which all cultivation unfolds.

To find this Gate is to enter the stream of return.

But to pass through it—to enter and dwell in the undivided—is the true challenge. It requires more than technique. It demands sincerity, virtue, humility, and clarity of heart. Because the Gate is not opened by effort—it opens itself to those who are aligned with it.

Beyond the Gate: The Final Return

From here, the last stages of the path unfold:

- The practitioner dissolves Qi into Hunran Yi Qi.

- Shen is returned to its Source.

- Even Emptiness is transcended.

- What remains is not a person, nor a state—but the Presence of Dao, unspoken and unconditioned.

And thus, the verse is fulfilled:

"Mystery of Mysteries — the Gate of All Marvelous and Subtle."

玄之又玄，眾妙之門。

This Gate is always here, but invisible to those who rush. It is always open, but closed to those who cling. It does not shine, yet lights the entire world.

Find it not by seeking—but by becoming still. Then you may begin to walk the return.

Appendices

Feedback on the Carpathian Retreat

By Alex Karmazin

When I first planned to attend a traditional-style retreat, I was a little nervous. At that time, my daily meditations were under two hours, and I had only been practicing for about a year. But once I arrived, the beauty of the Carpathian Mountains immediately dissolved all my worries. I had been to the Carpathians before, but never so far from civilization. The building where we stayed was the only one in the area — you'd need a serious pickup truck to even get there.

That first night, I had a clear sense: unless I aligned myself with Dao and opened fully to Heaven and Earth, resistance would only bring trouble. I tried to clear my mind and relax.

The first meditation was excellent. Outdoor meditations and Zhan Zhuang always seem to go deeper than those done indoors. After that first session, I felt I could have continued sitting for much longer, which gave me confidence and optimism. Later that night, as I lay in bed, I saw a flash of light. At first, I thought it might be a lantern or camera flash — but it was completely silent, and everyone else was already asleep. The flash came again, and then a third time. It was a strange and subtle experience.

One day, Vitaly introduced a technique for synchronizing the three Dantian. As I sat in meditation and began observing the process with inner vision, I noticed an incredible increase in detail compared to previous practices. At one point, I saw two pulsing channels in the Lower Dantian. They would expand and shrink to the size of a thread, and sometimes, I could feel Qi flowing through them like a glowing ball. What amazed me most was that these processes were happening naturally, without any conscious direction from me.

I repeated the practice the next day, this time including the Upper Dantian. Since I was only at the third level during this retreat, my Upper Dantian had not been fully activated. The Qi between the Middle and Upper Dantian was barely flowing — like trying to carve a new road through an overgrown field. It took a great deal of effort, but by the end of the session, I was able to establish a relatively smooth flow between the two.

At this point, the days and events started blending together in my memory. So from here on, I'll just describe the most vivid experiences.

One meditation took me much deeper than before. Until then, I had experienced my Qi as a glowing, chaotic mass. This time, I sensed it as a unified whole — one coherent presence that not only moved on its own but also responded to my influence.

In another session, I felt myself dissolve into nature. Something began to crystallize in the Dantian. The previously chaotic Qi started to take on a stable, unified structure — solid, coherent.

During an evening meditation focused on connecting with the stars, I experienced a powerful descending current. As I attuned myself to Heaven and Earth, a rush of Qi from above entered the crown of my head. I consciously shifted into a more spiritual and loving state, and the energy softened into a warm, downward flow. Even after the session ended, the energy remained strong. Following Vitaly's suggestion, I repeated the closing steps and gathered the Qi into the Dantian, gradually calming and consolidating the experience.

In the next session, something shifted. I no longer experienced my Lower Dantian as a flat or two-dimensional area. It now appeared as a full 3D sphere — a ball of Qi. The Qi wasn't evenly distributed, but I could now perceive its volume, density, and form more clearly. This was a completely new experience for me.

Another evening practice went unusually deep. I began with cultivating silence and calmness, letting the darkness settle around me. This helped me establish a deeper connection with the stars and planets. As the practice deepened, I became aware of my Lower Dantian — but my body seemed to disappear. My sense of internal Qi and the surrounding world merged into one continuum. The usual boundary between inner and outer dissolved. Though I didn't fully dissolve — thoughts and an observing mind were still present — it was a powerful, eye-opening moment of unity.

As that session concluded, one clear thought came into my mind: Say goodbye to this place. It felt a bit strange since I still had another day and one more meditation to go. But I followed the feeling and quietly said my farewell, taking a small piece of this place with me in my heart. The next day, it rained, and we didn't return to that spot again. Then the retreat ended, and I left.

This retreat was one of the most profound experiences of my life so far.

12 Meridians and

Their Correlations

The Heart Meridian

Phase: Fire

Direction: South

Season: Summer

Climate: Heat

Cultivation: Growth

Sense Organ: Tongue

Sense: Touch

Tissue: Vessels

Positive Emotion: Love, Joy

Negative Emotion: Hate, Arrogance

Flavor: Bitter

Sound: Laughter

Smell: Scorched

Time: 11 a.m. – 1 p.m.

Opposite: Gall Bladder

Yin/Yang: Yin

Flow Direction: Up

Origin/Ending: Chest to Hand

Number of Acupoints: 9

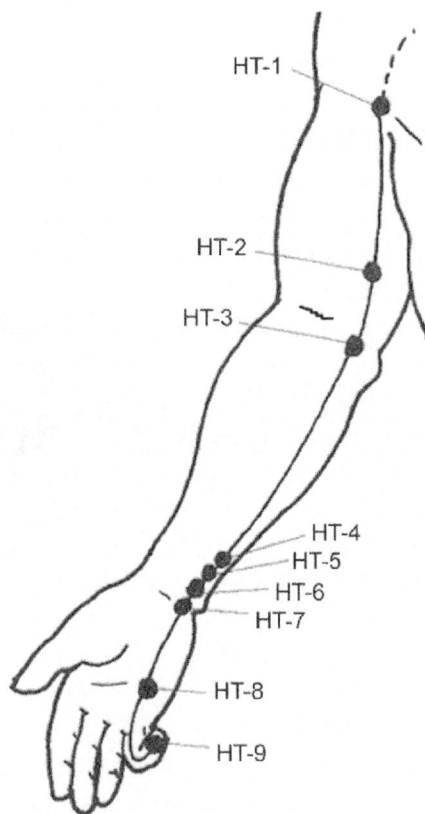

HT-1

HT-2

HT-3

HT-4
HT-5
HT-6
HT-7

HT-8

HT-9

The Lung Meridian

Phase: Metal

Direction: West

Season: Autumn

Climate: Dry

Cultivation: Reaping

Sense Organ: Nose

Sense: Smell

Tissue: Skin and Hair

Positive Emotion: Courage, Justice

Negative Emotion: Grief

Flavor: Pungent

Sound: Crying

Smell: Rotten

Time: 3 a.m. – 5 a.m.

Opposite: Bladder

Yin/Yang: Yin

Flow Direction: Up

Origin/Ending: Chest to Hand

Number of Acupoints: 11

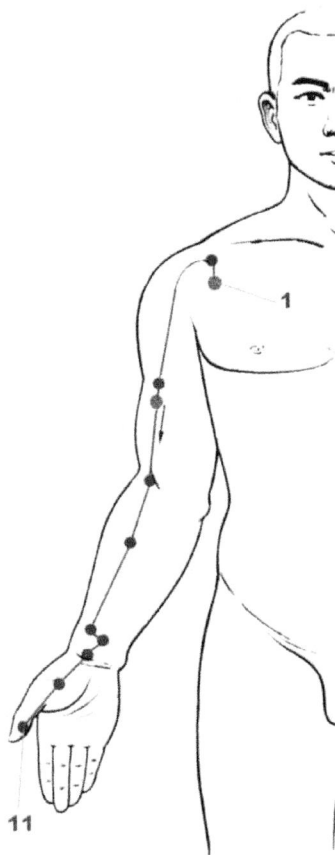

The Stomach Meridian

Phase: Earth

Direction: Center

Season: Late Summer

Climate: Damp

Cultivation: Transforming

Sense Organ: Mouth

Sense: Taste

Tissue: Muscles

Positive Emotion: Compassion, Sympathy

Negative Emotion: Anxiety

Flavor: Sweet

Sound: Singing

Smell: Fragrant

Time: 7 a.m. – 9 a.m.

Opposite: Pericardium

Yin/Yang: Yang

Flow Direction: Down

Origin/Ending: Face to Foot

Number of Acupoints: 45

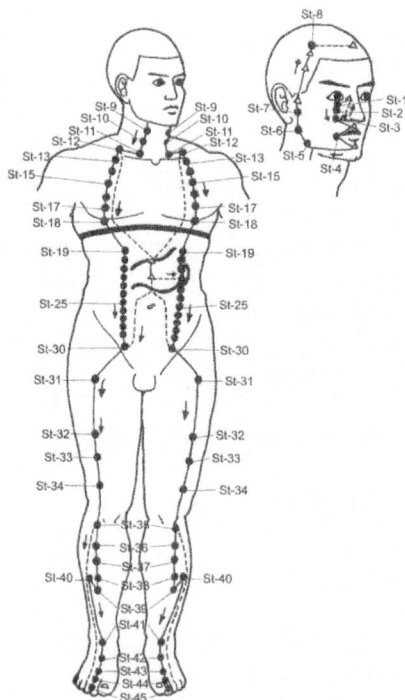

The Kidney Meridian

Phase: Water

Direction: North

Season: Winter

Climate: Cold

Cultivation: Hibernate

Sense Organ: Ears

Sense: Hearing

Tissue: Bones

Positive Emotion: Gentleness, Tenderness

Negative Emotion: Fear

Flavor: Salty

Sound: Groaning

Smell: Putrid

Time: 7 p.m. – 9 p.m.

Opposite: Large Intestine

Yin/Yang: Yin

Flow Direction: Up

Origin/Ending: Foot to Chest

Number of Acupoints: 27

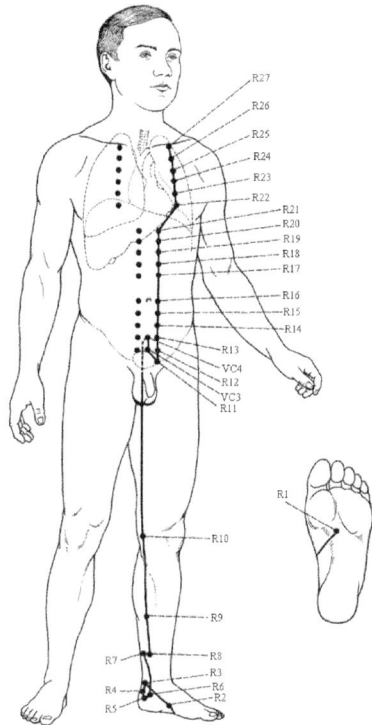

The Large Intestine Meridian

Phase: Metal

Direction: West

Season: Autumn

Climate: Dry

Cultivation: Reaping

Sense Organ: Nose

Sense: Smell

Tissue: Skin and Hair

Positive Emotion: Courage, Justice

Negative Emotion: Grief

Flavor: Pungent

Sound: Crying

Smell: Rotten

Time: 5 a.m. – 7 a.m.

Opposite: Kidney

Yin/Yang: Yang

Flow Direction: Down

Origin/Ending: Hand to Face

Number of Acupoints: 20

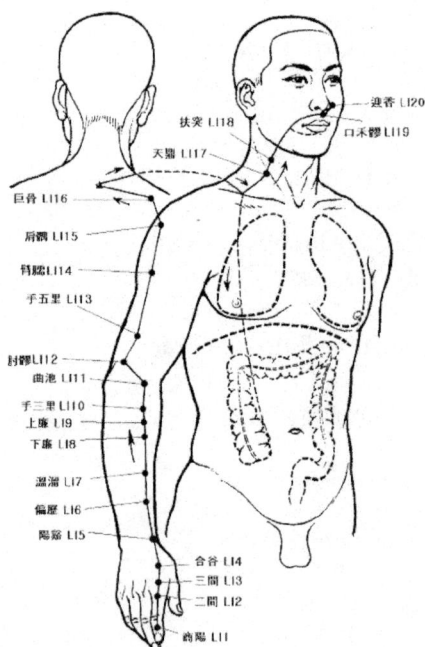

The Small Intestine Meridian

Phase: Fire

Direction: South

Season: Summer

Climate: Heat

Cultivation: Growth

Sense Organ: Tongue

Sense: Touch

Tissue: Blood, Arteries, Veins

Positive Emotion: Love, Joy

Negative Emotion: Hate, Arrogance

Flavor: Bitter

Sound: Laughter

Smell: Scorched

Time: 1 p.m. – 3 p.m.

Opposite: Liver

Yin/Yang: Yang

Flow Direction: Down

Origin/Ending: Hand to Face

Number of Acupoints: 19

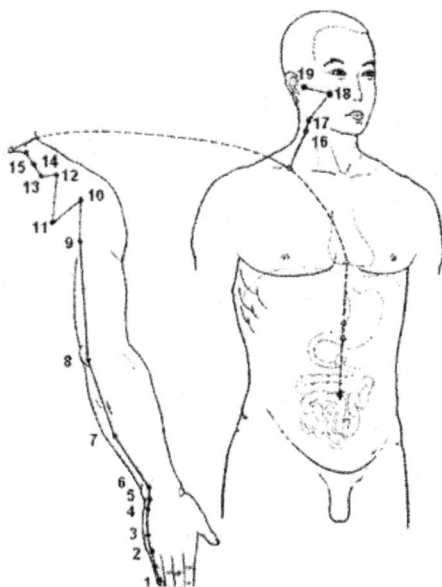

The Liver Meridian

Phase: Wood

Direction: East

Season: Spring

Climate: Windy

Cultivation: Germinate

Sense Organ: Eyes

Sense: Sight

Tissue: Tendons

Positive Emotion: Kindness

Negative Emotion: Anger

Flavor: Sour

Sound: Shouting

Smell: Scorched

Time: 1 a.m. – 3 a.m.

Opposite: Small Intestine

Yin/Yang: Yin

Flow Direction: Up

Origin/Ending: Foot to Chest

Number of Acupoints: 14

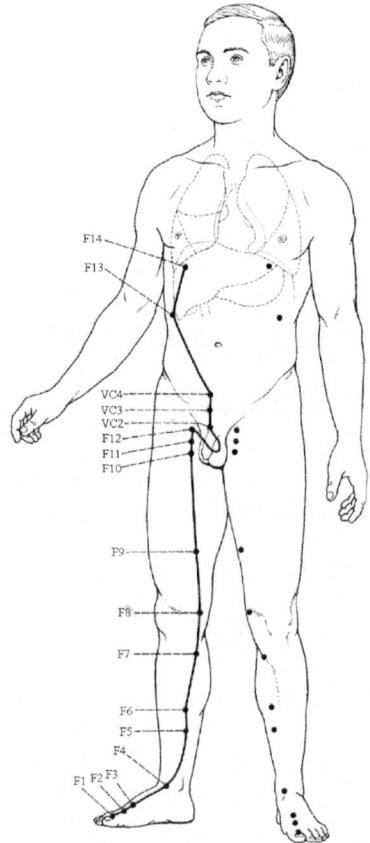

The Bladder Meridian

Phase: Water

Direction: North

Season: Winter

Climate: Cold

Cultivation: Hibernate

Sense Organ: Ears

Sense: Hearing

Tissue: Bones

Positive Emotion: Gentleness, Tenderness

Negative Emotion: Fear

Flavor: Salty

Sound: Groaning

Smell: Putrid

Time: 3 p.m. – 5 p.m.

Opposite: Lung

Yin / Yang: Yang

Flow Direction: Down

Origin / Ending: Face to Foot

Number of Acupoints: 67

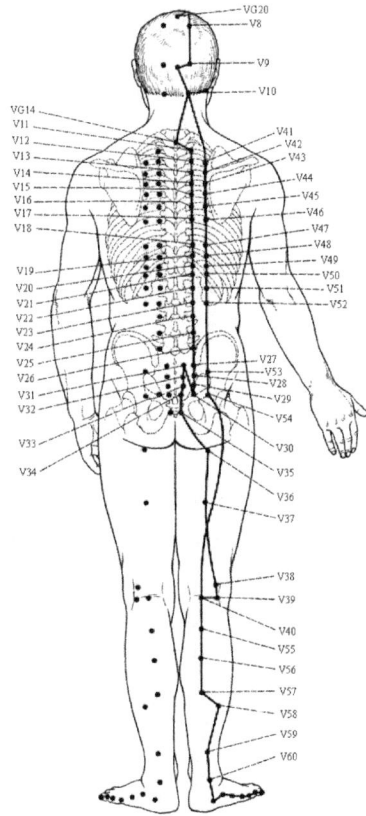

The Gallbladder Meridian

Phase: Wood

Direction: East

Season: Spring

Climate: Windy

Cultivation: Germinate

Sense Organ: Eyes

Sense: Sight

Tissue: Tendons

Positive Emotion: Kindness

Negative Emotion: Anger

Flavor: Sour

Sound: Shouting

Smell: Scorched

Time: 11 p.m. -1 a.m.

Opposite: Heart

Yin/Yang: Yang

Flow Direction: Down

Origin/Ending: Face to Foot

Number of Acupoints: 44

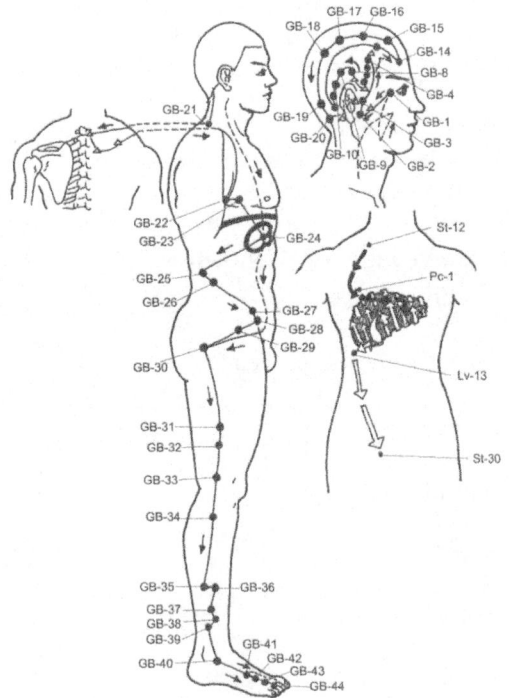

The Spleen Meridian

Phase: Earth

Direction: Center

Season: Late Summer

Climate: Damp

Cultivation: Transforming

Sense Organ: Mouth

Sense: Taste

Tissue: Muscles

Positive Emotion: Sympathy, Compassion

Negative Emotion: Anxiety

Flavor: Sweet

Sound: Singing

Smell: Fragrant

Time: 9 a.m. – 11 a.m.

Opposite: Triple Warmer

Yin/Yang: Yin

Flow Direction: Up

Origin/Ending: Foot to Chest

Number of Acupoints: 21

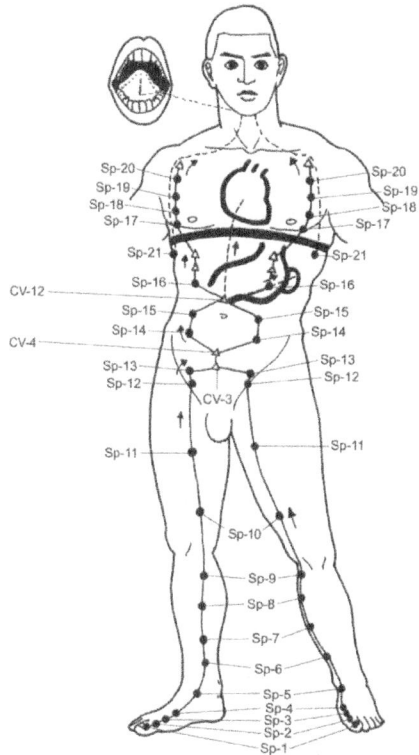

The Pericardium Meridian

Phase: Fire

Direction: South

Season: Summer

Climate: Heat

Cultivation: Growth

Sense Organ: Tongue

Sense: Touch

Tissue: Blood, Arteries, Veins

Positive Emotion: Love, Joy

Negative Emotion: Arrogance, Hate

Flavor: Bitter

Sound: Laughter

Smell: Scorched

Time: 7 p.m. – 9 p.m.

Opposite: Stomach

Yin/Yang: Yin

Flow Direction: Up

Origin/Ending: Chest to Hand

Number of Acupoints: 9

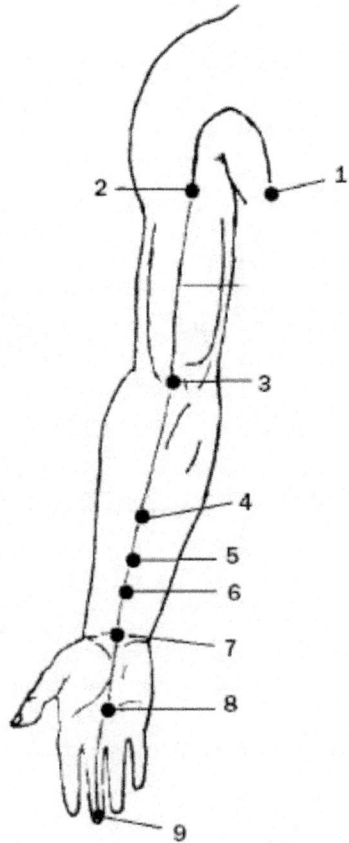

The Triple-Warmer Meridian

Phase: Fire

Direction: South

Season: Summer

Climate: Heat

Cultivation: Growth

Sense Organ: Tongue

Sense: Touch

Tissue: Blood, Arteries, Veins

Positive Emotion: Love, Joy

Negative Emotion: Hate, Arrogance

Flavor: Bitter

Sound: Laughter

Smell: Scorched

Time: 9 p.m. – 11 p.m.

Opposite: Spleen

Yin / Yang: Yang

Flow Direction: Down

Origin / Ending: Hand to Face

Number of Acupoints: 23

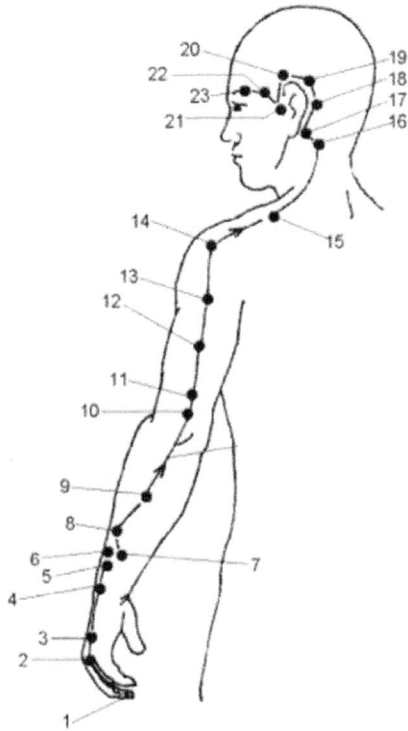

Daoist Cultivation, Book 2 Cultivation of the Original Nature - Xing Gong: The essential work for Qigong, Neigong and Neidan

This second volume in the Daoist Cultivation series focuses on one of the most essential dimensions of Daoist practice: **Xing Gong**, the cultivation of Original Nature.

It offers practical guidance and insight into key aspects of inner development:

- The purification of the heart–mind from emotional and mental impurities

- The cultivation of Virtue (德, dé) as the ground of true transformation

- The gradual dissolution of ignorance and delusion through sincere practice

A dedicated chapter on **"Obstacles and Distractions"** helps practitioners recognize common inner hindrances and provides advice rooted in classical wisdom.

This book also explores the profound process of **Entering the Gate**, including:

- The Signs of a True Teacher

- The Qualities of a Sincere Student

- The Teacher–Disciple Bond and the Meaning of Initiation

- Inner Markers of the Genuine Path

It features selected translations from classical Daoist texts— including teachings by Wang Chongyang and Zhang Sanfeng—as well as two rare works:

- Lao Jun Exalts One Hundred Medicines – a verse text on cultivating spiritual virtues

- Lao Jun Speaks About One Hundred Diseases – a mirror of karmic habits and inner afflictions

This book is both a philosophical guide and a hands-on manual, offering powerful tools to help modern practitioners return to clarity, simplicity, and the luminous stillness of their Original Nature.

Daoist Cultivation, Book 3
Ming Gong: Qigong, Neigong and Neidan: 1st Level of Inner Alchemy + Video

This volume offers a practical and profound gateway into the living tradition of Daoist Internal Alchemy (Neidan, 內丹). Focusing on Ming Gong (命功)—the Cultivation of Life-Essence—this book provides step-by-step guidance in the foundational physical and energetic methods of Daoist practice, including:
- "Gathering the Qi of Heaven and Nature" (採天地之氣) – harmonizing with the natural forces to nourish vitality
- "Daoist Breathing Techniques" (道家吐納法) – cultivating Zhen Qi (真氣, genuine qi) through conscious breath
- "Zhan Zhuang" (站樁) – standing meditation to unify body, breath, and intention according to Daoist teachings.
- and other core Qigong and Neigong techniques that awaken, refine, and direct internal energy

At the heart of this book lies the first stage of Neidan, where practice transitions from basic energy work to inner transformation. Key methods include:

- "Stabilizing the Furnace and Setting Up the Cauldron" (安爐立鼎) – preparing the internal environment for alchemical refinement
- "Collecting the Ingredients" (採藥) – gathering the essential substances within the body and Qi system
- "Elixir Cultivation" (煉丹) – initiating the subtle inner fire to produce the inner elixir

This book also explains how Zong Qi (宗氣), Ying Qi (營氣), Wei Qi (衛氣), and Gu Qi (谷氣) are forming Zheng Qi (正氣, Upright Qi), the purified and upright energetic force necessary for deeper alchemical change.

What sets this book apart is its illumination of the subtle art of Xing Gong (性功)—the Cultivation of Original Nature—as an inseparable part of each Ming Gong method. True internal cultivation is not merely the circulation of energy but the simultaneous purification of the heart–mind and return to inner stillness.

Within every breath and movement lies the opportunity to gather: Calmness (靜, jìng) and Quietness (清, qīng) from Heaven and Nature - These essential spiritual qualities are often overlooked, yet they form the gateway to perceiving and connecting with Ling Qi (靈氣)—the spiritual resonance that links the practitioner with the Primordial Dao

To support your personal journey, this book includes:
- Clear, photo-illustrated step-by-step instructions for each practice
- An exclusive YouTube video playlist, allowing you to visually follow and embody the teachings in a safe and accurate way

Whether you are just beginning your exploration of Daoist cultivation or are a serious practitioner deepening your Neidan practice, this book will serve as a reliable companion and guide. Rooted in the classical principles, yet clearly structured for modern use, it opens the door to authentic transformation—of body, Qi, and spirit.

Daoist Cultivation, Book 4
The Classic: 24 Essential Instructions for Disciples - Translation and Commentary

This book presents a clear and accessible translation of the classic Daoist text "Twenty-Four Essential Instructions for Disciples" by the renowned Inner Alchemy master Liu Yiming.

As with many traditional Daoist writings, the original text is composed in a highly refined and symbolic style—profound, but often difficult for modern readers to fully grasp. To make these teachings more approachable, this translation is accompanied by insightful commentary that explains each of the twenty-four instructions in clear and practical language, while preserving their original depth.

Why is this text important?

Liu Yiming himself answers that question:

"These twenty-four essential instructions mentioned above are crucial gates and key points that you must put into practice. You have to go through all of them, accept, understand, and realize each one; only then will you be able to meet the True Teacher and hear about the Great Dao. If there is even one instruction that you cannot realize and practice, even if you meet the True Teacher and hear about the Dao, the result will be unpredictable and may possibly lead nowhere."

This book is an invaluable guide for serious practitioners of Daoist cultivation, especially those walking the path of Neidan (inner alchemy). It bridges the gap between ancient instruction and modern understanding—opening the gates, step by step, toward true realization of the Dao.

Daoist Cultivation, Book 5
Elixir Cultivation: Qigong, Neigong and Neidan - Second Level + Video

This volume is the second part of a practical guide to traditional Daoist cultivation, continuing the step-by-step approach introduced in earlier books. Here, you'll find an authentic and detailed presentation of foundational Ming Gong techniques, rooted in classical training methods.

The book offers in-depth instruction on Qigong and Neigong practices, not only for supporting health but also as essential components of Inner Alchemy (Neidan). Practices include:

- "Dynamic Attunement to Nature"
- "Improving Qi Circulation in the Arm Meridians"
- "Zhan Zhuang – Second Level"
- And other methods for deepening internal cultivation

You will also continue exploring the process of Elixir Formation, with advanced stages such as:

- Middle Dantian Cultivation
- Zhong Mai (Central Channel) Cultivation
- Integration of the Zhong Mai and Two Dantians
- Small Heavenly Circulation — including the traditional opening of the Du Mai and Ren Mai channels

This book also includes a translation of the classic Daoist text: "Wondrous Scripture for the Daily Internal Practice of the Great Taishang Lao Jun"—a rare and powerful teaching on consistent inner refinement.

To support your learning, the book includes:

- Instructional photos for key exercises
- A link to an exclusive YouTube video playlist, so you can follow along with correct form and technique

Daoist Cultivation, Book 6
Chapters on Awakening to the True Reality: The Daoist Classic

This second edition of Awakening to the True Reality by Zhang Boduan (《悟真篇》) presents the first complete English translation of one of Daoism's most essential works on internal alchemy (內丹, nèidān). Traditionally attributed to the Song dynasty adept Zhang Boduan (張伯端), the Wu Zhen Pian has guided generations of Daoist practitioners on the subtle process of refining Essence, cultivating Qi, and returning to the Original Spirit.

Building on the first edition, this expanded version offers greater precision, textual fidelity, and structural completeness. The entire classical Chinese text is included alongside a refined, line-by-line English translation. Each verse is accompanied by detailed commentary grounded in traditional Neidan doctrine, designed to clarify the symbolic language and alchemical transformations at the heart of Zhang Boduan's teaching.

This edition also restores and explains the traditional structure of the *Wu Zhen Pian*, including:

- The **Preface** (前序), setting forth Zhang Boduan's intentions;
- The **Diagram of the Elixir Chamber's Precious Mirror** (丹房寶鑑之圖), a symbolic image included in several influential later transmissions;
- The **Sixteen Regulated Quatrains** (七言四韻一十六首), based on the symbolic number 二八一斤;
- The **Sixty-Four Verses** (七言絕句六十四首), corresponding to the hexagrams of the *Book of Changes* (周易);
- A series of **symbolic lyric poems**, including *Twelve Verses in the Tune of "Moon over the West River"* (西江月十二首), one **Additional Verse** (又一首) representing the intercalary month, and **Five Quatrains** (絕句五首) symbolizing the Five Phases (五行);
- The **Afterword** (後序), reflecting on the purpose and limitations of transmission.

In addition, this second edition includes new **Appendices and Supplementary Verses** that expand upon Zhang Boduan's teachings and place them in the broader context of Daoist inner alchemy. These additional texts—**included in some traditional editions of the *Wu Zhen Pian***—provide further insight into symbolic correspondences, cosmological patterns, and the oral transmission lineages that shaped this classic text's reception over the centuries.

Designed for both committed practitioners and readers seeking deeper insight into Daoist inner transformation, this edition remains faithful to the classical phrasing while offering accessible guidance through its layered wisdom. Whether approached as a sacred scripture, a spiritual manual, or a philosophical work, the *Wu Zhen Pian* continues to reveal new depths to those who read with clarity, sincerity, and perseverance.

Daoist Cultivation, Book 7
Alchemical Principles: Twenty-Four Secret Instructions for Disciples by Liu Yiming

This second edition of *Daoist Cultivation, Book 7: Alchemical Principles – Twenty-Four Secret Instructions for Disciples by Liu Yiming* presents a carefully revised and expanded version of the original work, deepening its clarity, structure, and contemplative resonance.

In this edition, the twenty-four essential instructions by Liu Yiming (劉一明) — one of the great masters of Daoist internal alchemy (Neidan) — are now integrated into a complete cultivation cycle. Each instruction is paired with a comprehensive commentary, followed by an original poetic verse from the *Collected Songs of Silent Cultivation in the Way of the Elixir* (丹道靜修歌集). These verses, written in the Daoist tradition, echo and express the heart of each teaching through symbolic and intuitive language.

The second edition introduces a new feature: Silent Ripening Style commentary. These meditative reflections follow each song and distill the inner meaning of the chapter in a tone of quiet guidance, allowing the teaching to resonate beyond the words. Each chapter also concludes with a Daoist Terms Table, offering clear definitions, Chinese characters, and pinyin for all essential concepts.

This edition refines the structure of the book into a rhythm of study and contemplation:

1. Liu Yiming's original instruction

2. In-depth commentary on the instruction

3. Matching cultivation song

4. Silent Ripening Style commentary on the song

5. Glossary of key Daoist terms

The second edition also benefits from improved translations, refined language, and enhanced consistency in the presentation of Daoist terminology, symbolism, and cosmology. It is intended not only as a text for study, but as a living manual for serious practitioners of the Way.

Daoist Cultivation, Book 8: Dao De Jing by Lao Zi

Dao De Jing is the most well-known Daoist classic, attributed to Laozi and written approximately 2,300 to 2,500 years ago. With so many translations already available, you might ask: *Why offer another one?*

Here's why I created this translation.

After I shared a passage on Daoist breathing techniques from my Book 1 on Facebook, someone responded by citing *Dao De Jing*, Chapter 55, claiming it "explicitly warns against interfering with the breath." I explained that this was a misunderstanding—that breathing techniques are indeed part of traditional Daoist practice. The commenter referred to the Gia-Fu Feng translation. When I checked it, I found the line: *"Controlling the breath causes strain."*

But when I examined the original Chinese, I realized something important: the character used was 氣 **(Qì)**—not "breath," but **Qi**, the fundamental energy in Daoist cultivation. The translation was not only inaccurate, it also contradicted the spirit of the entire chapter, which praises the power and vitality of someone aligned with the Dao.

The original phrase—心使氣曰強—means *"Using the mind–heart to direct Qi is called strength."* This expresses something quite different. Despite there being over a hundred English versions of the *Dao De Jing,* many introduce distortions or misrepresentations. I didn't review every one, but I realized the only way to be sure was to translate it myself.

If you're seeking more than just a translation—if you want deep commentary rooted in the principles of Neidan (Internal Alchemy) —you'll find it in Book 15 of this series: *Dao De Jing: The Dao of Inner Alchemy – A Neidan Guide to the Classic of the Way and Virtue.*

Daoist Cultivation, Book 9

Collection: 15 Discourses by Wang Chongyang, Qingjing Jing, Yinfu Jing

This volume presents a carefully selected collection of essential Daoist texts—scriptures that every serious follower of the Dao should know and reflect upon throughout their cultivation journey. The texts included are:

- "Fifteen Discourses Establishing the Teaching" by Wang Chongyang
- "Qingjing Jing" (Scripture on Clarity and Stillness)
- "Huangdi Yinfu Jing" (Scripture on Hidden Talismans by the Yellow Emperor)

Fifteen Discourses Establishing the Teaching

This important text by Wang Chongyang, one of the great figures of Daoist history, is presented with full commentary. Each discourse is carefully explained to illuminate the deeper meanings and practical implications of the original teachings. Every detail of the text has been unpacked to serve modern practitioners walking the inner path.

Qingjing Jing

Often called the *Scripture on Clarity and Stillness*, the Qingjing Jing is one of the most profound texts in the Daoist canon—yet remains far less known in the West compared to the *Dao De Jing*. Although short in length, it contains extraordinary insight into the nature of mind, stillness, and the Dao. This edition includes a faithful translation with select footnotes for clarity and context.

Huangdi Yinfu Jing

Translated as the *Scripture on Hidden Talismans* or *The Secret Correspondences of the Yellow Emperor*, this text reveals the subtle patterns between Heaven, Earth, and Human Life. There are two known versions of the *Yinfu Jing*—a shorter one with just over 300 characters, and a longer one, divided into three sections, with over 400 characters.
This translation presents the complete longer version, with additional footnotes to support your reading.

This collection is designed not for passive reading, but for active contemplation. It is meant to accompany your inner work, offering wisdom, depth, and clarity from some of Daoism's most revered texts and voices.

Daoist Cultivation, Book 10
Retreat Program: + Translation of Wang Chongyang's text

This Second Edition offers a refined and expanded guide to conducting a traditional Daoist retreat—an essential phase of dedicated practice for those walking the inner path.

Whether you're preparing for your first period of seclusion or seeking to deepen your solitary cultivation, this updated edition provides both clear structure and deeper insight, grounded in authentic Daoist principles of internal refinement and withdrawal from worldly distractions.

Inside, you will find practical answers to key retreat questions, such as:
– How to choose the right retreat environment
– What to prepare before entering retreat
– A general daily schedule for balanced practice
– How to regulate the heart–mind during withdrawal
– Specific methods and practices to focus on during the retreat

What's new in this Second Edition:
– A Flexible Home Retreat Schedule for those cultivating in everyday settings
– A thoroughly revised translation of the classic Quanzhen text: *The Twenty-Four Essential Instructions Transmitted by the True Man Chongyang to Master Danyang*
– Clearer explanations and updated language throughout the retreat guide
– Improved layout and formatting for easier use in practice settings

Included Text:
At the end of the book is a new and refined translation of *The Twenty-Four Essential Instructions*, a core transmission text in the Quanzhen tradition. Rich with alchemical meaning, this rare work offers deep insight into the subtle inner principles of Daoist cultivation and complements the retreat teachings with authentic wisdom.

Whether used to plan a dedicated period of retreat or to deepen your ongoing training, this Second Edition supports your journey into the quiet heart of Daoist practice—whether in the mountains or in the stillness of your own home.

Daoist Cultivation, Book 11
Zhang Sanfeng: The Daoist Classic - Translation and Commentary

This newly expanded second edition includes three classical texts traditionally associated with the legendary Daoist master Zhang Sanfeng—mystic, alchemist, and teacher of the inner Way:

- *Speaking of the Dao in Simple Words*

- *Song of Meditation*

- *Ninefold Dao Ballad* (九更道情)

All texts are presented with detailed commentary, exploring both practical teachings and symbolic dimensions. Where needed, the original Chinese is provided alongside insights into how terms were translated and interpreted. The first text, *Speaking of the Dao in Simple Words*, has again been divided into thematic sections with added titles for clarity, allowing easier navigation through its many layered topics.

This second edition also includes:

- A new preface and postface contextualizing Zhang Sanfeng's contribution to Daoist thought

- A discussion of the authorship of the Ninefold Dao Ballad, including its transmission history and thematic links to inner alchemy

- An appendix featuring two original song collections:

    ◦ *The Flower Blooms at the Mysterious Gate* (花開玄門)

    ◦ *The Nine Stages of Returning to the Real* (還真九階)
    These poetic works, inspired by Daoist principles,

trace the inner transformation from delusion to realization. The first is accompanied by commentary in the Silent Ripening Style.

Whether you are a long-time student of Daoist cultivation or discovering Zhang Sanfeng's teachings for the first time, this volume offers a refined and accessible entry point into the timeless wisdom of the Dao.

Daoist Cultivation, Book 12
The Secret of the Golden Flower: Translation and Commentary

The Secret of the Golden Flower is one of the most widely known Daoist texts in the West. It offers a symbolic and meditative description of Daoist Inner Alchemy, blending influences from Daoism, Buddhism, and Confucianism into a cohesive inner tradition.

This edition presents a complete and faithful translation of the entire text—including chapters 9 through 13, which were missing from Richard Wilhelm's original 1929 translation.

To support your understanding, the text is accompanied by extensive commentary, clarifying difficult terms and symbolic imagery, and explaining why certain translation choices were made. This book is designed for modern readers with a sincere interest in authentic Daoist cultivation.

About Earlier Translations:

The first translation by Richard Wilhelm, accompanied by commentary from Carl Gustav Jung, played a major role in introducing the text to the West. However, it contains numerous mistranslations and interpretive errors, and omits the final five chapters of the original work. As a result, Jung's psychological commentary—while historically interesting—is not aligned with the actual principles of Daoist inner alchemy.

A later translation by Thomas Cleary improved the flow and readability but replaces traditional Daoist terminology with more modern or abstract equivalents. For example, Yin and Yang are rendered as "negative energy" and "positive energy," which significantly narrows their meaning. Some key passages were also paraphrased or omitted entirely.

What This Version Offers:

- A complete translation of the original text, including chapters absent in earlier versions
- Preservation of core Daoist terms such as *Yin, Yang, Qi, Shen*, and more
- In-depth commentary clarifying key symbols, phrases, and practices
- Contextual insight into the alchemical, meditative, and spiritual dimensions of the work

This version of *The Secret of the Golden Flower* is intended for readers who wish to move beyond poetic mysticism or psychological metaphor and step into the depth of actual Daoist cultivation.

Daoist Cultivation, Book 13
The Art of Sleeping

This revised and expanded second edition of Daoist Cultivation, Book 13: The Art of Sleeping presents a complete and carefully integrated system of Shui Gong (睡功)—the ancient Daoist practice of sleep-based cultivation and inner alchemical dreaming.

Building on the foundational teachings of Inner Alchemy (內丹, nèidān), this edition includes:

- Refined translations of classical texts by Chen Tuan, Zhang Sanfeng, Lü Dongbin, Wang Daoyuan, and other Daoist masters, capturing the subtle meanings and poetic nuance of the originals.

- Line-by-line commentary on all texts presented in the book, offering a step-by-step guide to sleep-based cultivation.

- Clear distinction between Ordinary Dreams, Lucid Dreams, and True Dreams, grounded in Daoist cosmology and spirit physiology.

- New instructional chapters on pre-sleep posture, whole-body breathing, intention-setting, and returning with clarity.

- Insightful integration of concepts like Yuan Shen (元神), Hun and Po Souls (魂魄), and the principle of "Desire without desire" (有意無意).

This edition is intended for practitioners who already have a foundation in the Daoist path—especially those familiar with Xing Gong (性功) and Elixir Cultivation as presented in Books 1–3 of this series. It is not a dreamwork manual in the modern psychological sense, but a gateway into the profound spiritual uses of the sleep state as practiced in traditional Daoist inner alchemy.

Daoist Cultivation, Book 14
Discourse on Sitting in Forgetfulness: Translation and Commentary

This edition of Discourse on Sitting in Forgetfulness (坐忘論, Zuò Wàng Lùn) presents a complete and carefully compiled version of the classic Daoist text by Sīmǎ Chéngzhēn (司馬承禎), a leading Tang dynasty master of the Shangqing tradition. Drawing from both major manuscript traditions, this volume includes:

- The full seven chapters of the main treatise

- The complete Preface by Sīmǎ Chéngzhēn

- The Preface by Hermit Zhēn Jìng

The concluding chapter Pivot and Wings of Sitting in Forgetfulness—a key summary of the supporting methods that help stabilize and elevate practice

Together, these materials provide a comprehensive map for Daoist meditation, virtue cultivation, and inner transformation. The text outlines a step-by-step progression: from establishing faith and reverence, to releasing karmic entanglements, calming the heart–mind, observing reality clearly, entering Profound Stillness and Calmness (定, Ding), and finally attaining unity with the Dao.

Sīmǎ Chéngzhēn's teaching integrates insights from Daoism, Confucianism, and Buddhism, reflecting a deep harmony between ethical conduct, mental purification, and metaphysical realization.

This edition includes detailed commentary on the text itself, clarifying difficult passages, unpacking classical references, and guiding the reader through essential terms such as Original Wisdom (慧), True Observation (真觀). It also notes subtle differences between early manuscript versions and their implications for practice.

This refined second edition offers both scholarly depth and practical instruction. It is ideal for students of Daoist meditation, internal alchemy, and the classical path of returning to stillness, clarity, and the Way.

Daoist Cultivation, Book 15
Dao De Jing: The Dao of Inner Alchemy: A Neidan Guide to the Classic of the Way and Virtue

This is not a traditional commentary on the Dao De Jing. It is not academic, nor historical, nor philosophical in the usual sense. This book is a companion for those walking the inner path— a guide to the quiet work of Neidan, or inner alchemy.

Each chapter of the Dao De Jing is explored through the lens of Daoist cultivation, drawing out its deeper meaning as it applies to body, energy, heart-mind, and spirit.

Rather than focusing on outward moral teachings or abstract theory, this book follows the hidden thread of transformation— how the ancient words point toward stillness, softness, and the return to what is natural and whole within you.

You will find:

• Detailed Neidan (inner alchemy) readings rooted in classical Daoist cultivation

• Line-by-line breakdowns that unpack each verse's layers of paradox, imagery, and insight

- A balance of poetic reflection and practical depth

- Explorations of Doing that returns to Non-Doing, and of emptiness that gives rise to power

Whether you're drawn to the Dao De Jing as poetry, as philosophy, or as a guide for inner transformation, this book offers something rare: a bridge between timeless depth and everyday clarity.

Daoist Cultivation, Book 16
Debates on the Cultivation of True Reality -
Translation and Commentary

A profound Daoist classic on inner transformation, self-cultivation, and the true meaning of the Golden Elixir.

Debates on the Cultivation of True Reality (《修真辯難》) is one of the most systematic and penetrating works in the Daoist internal alchemy (Neidan, 內丹) tradition. Attributed to Liu Yiming (1734–1821), a great master of the Quanzhen school, this text presents a rich series of over 120 question-and-answer exchanges between the adept Wuyuanzi and his disciples.

With clarity, precision, and depth, the dialogue explores every major aspect of Daoist cultivation—including the dual cultivation of Xìng (性, original nature) and Mìng (命, life-force), the refinement of Qì (氣, energy), the symbolic meaning of alchemical terms such as Lead and Mercury, and the proper method for forming the Golden Elixir (金丹). The format not only conveys doctrine, but preserves the feel of a living oral transmission—full of subtle warnings, sharp distinctions, and heartfelt guidance.

This edition includes:

- A complete and faithful English translation of the full text
- Xìng, Mìng, and Qì preserved in transliteration, with in-depth explanations
- Extensive commentary on the text, explaining passages and classical symbolism.
- A translator's introduction and a final reflection to support the reader's own path of cultivation

Written for serious students of Daoism as well as those curious about authentic inner alchemical teachings, this book serves as both a reference and a guide. It offers not shortcuts, but clarity—a mirror for the path, the practitioner, and the subtle workings of Heaven and Earth.

Daoist Cultivation, Book 17
Later Debates on the Cultivation of True Reality: Translation and Commentary

This book presents a complete and faithful translation of the classical Daoist text Later Debates on the Cultivation of True Reality (《修真後辯》), a profound continuation of the earlier work Debates on the Cultivation of Reality (《修真辯難》). Written in a clear and direct style, this later text deepens the exploration of Daoist internal alchemy (內丹, nèidān), correcting misunderstandings and offering practical insight into the authentic Way.

The text covers both foundational and advanced principles—discussing virtue, clarity of mind, gradual progression, and the true meaning behind alchemical metaphors such as Lead,

Mercury, and the Elixir. The work emphasizes the importance of sincerity, perseverance, and inner transformation over superficial methods or empty ambition.

Although rooted in a specific historical context, the warnings and corrections for students, offered in this text remain strikingly relevant for modern practitioners. It speaks directly to those who sincerely wish to refine their body, energy, and spirit in alignment with the Dao.

This edition includes:

- A complete, high-fidelity translation in refined English
- Extensive internal alchemical commentary in clear prose
- Clarification of common errors and subtle alchemical principles
- A formal introduction and final reflection on the work's meaning

Whether you are a student of Daoism, a serious cultivator, or a reader interested in classical wisdom, Later Debates on the Cultivation of True Reality offers a rare and valuable window into the heart of the internal path.

If you would like to continue exploring Daoism, you're welcome to follow my pages for updates, reflections, and resources:

Instagram https://www.instagram.com/daoist_cultivation

Facebook https://www.facebook.com/DaoismTaichiLosAngeles

If you have questions about Daoist philosophy, inner cultivation, or any of the practices mentioned in this book, feel free to reach out via direct message on either platform. I do my best to respond and clarify when I can.

For inquiries about group classes, private instruction, online consultations, or hosting a workshop in your city, please contact me through Instagram or Facebook.

I look forward to supporting your journey on the Path.

— *With respect and stillness,*
Vitaly Filbert

Daoist Cultivation Press

Los Angeles, CA, USA

Printed in Dunstable, United Kingdom